GUITAR
CHORD HANDBOOK

GUITAR
CHORD HANDBOOK

Over **500** illustrated chords for rock,
blues, soul, country, jazz, and classical

PHIL CAPONE

CHARTWELL
BOOKS

Inspiring | Educating | Creating | Entertaining

Brimming with creative inspiration, how-to projects, and useful information to enrich your everyday life, Quarto Knows is a favorite destination for those pursuing their interests and passions. Visit our site and dig deeper with our books into your area of interest: Quarto Creates, Quarto Cooks, Quarto Homes, Quarto Lives, Quarto Drives, Quarto Explores, Quarto Gifts, or Quarto Kids.

A QUARTO BOOK

This edition published in 2018 by Chartwell Books
an imprint of The Quarto Group,
142 West 36th Street, 4th Floor,
New York, NY 10018, USA
T (212) 779-4972 F (212) 779-6058
www.QuartoKnows.com

ISBN: 978-0-7858-3630-8

QUAR: 302815

Conceived, edited, and designed by
Quarto Publishing plc
an imprint of The Quarto Group
The Old Brewery
6 Blundell Street
London N7 9BH

Chartwell Books titles are also available at discount for retail, wholesale, promotional, and bulk purchase. For details, contact the Special Sales Manager by email at: specialsales@quarto.com or by mail at: The Quarto Group, Attn: Special Sales Manager, 401 Second Avenue North, Suite 310, Minneapolis, MN 55401, USA.

10 9 8 7 6 5 4 3 2 1

Printed in China

CONTENTS

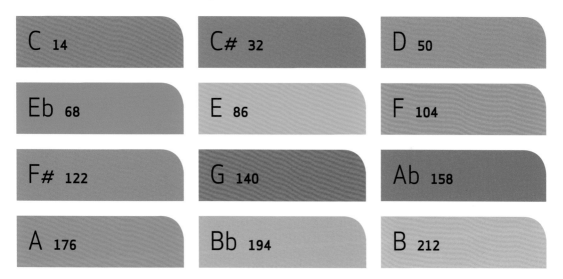

INTRODUCTION

The object of this book is to provide a complete, self-contained chord reference for guitarists at every level of ability; however, it is also an ideal aid for tutors who will hopefully find the logical and systematic concept of our "bible" very helpful in many teaching scenarios. In fact, during my many years of teaching guitar, I have frequently been asked by students which chord book they should buy, and frankly, there are none that I have felt I could whole-heartedly recommended—hence the birth of this wonderful book.

Organized into keys and ascending chromatically from C to B, there are five different chord shapes for all of the commonly encountered chord types in each key. These five shapes span the entire fingerboard and so work on many levels—the student being free to choose the most manageable voicing, the more experienced player picking a chord for ease of change in a sequence, or perhaps to provide a greater choice of harmonic texture in an accompaniment.

The supplementary section, while not intended to provide a comprehensive reference, will nonetheless provide a useful resource for those situations when stylized chords from specific genres are required, and includes the more frequently used chords types from the worlds of rock, blues, jazz, soul, funk, and reggae. All this content is wrapped in a very "user-friendly" package with clear labeling, color coding, and a photograph of every chord shape supplementing the standard chord box format.

The book has been designed with travel in mind—the compact dimensions allow the book to fit easily into your guitar case or gig bag. Happy practicing!

HOW TO USE THIS BOOK

This glossary of icons and symbols has been designed to enhance your learning experience by enabling you to get the chords off the page and onto your guitar as quickly as possible.

Features

1 TITLE The key (e.g. E) and chord type (e.g. MAJOR) appear at the top of every unit. Chords are grouped into three basic chord types: major, minor, and dominant seventh (7).

2 INTRODUCTION A short description of the chord, giving an insight into the sound, voicing and position of the chord. Well-known uses of particular chords are commented on here.

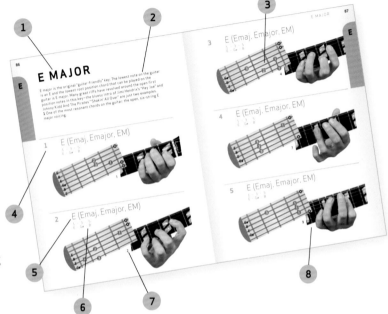

3 FINGERBOARD DIAGRAM Each chord is clearly annotated on a chord box with color-coded symbols indicating fingering and root-note location.

4 CHORD NUMBERING Each chord is numbered from one to five, with one being the lowest available voicing and five being the highest available voicing. This allows for a quick selection of chords required in a specific area of the fingerboard (or fretboard).

5 CHORD SUB-HEADING The chord type is described in more harmonic detail (e.g. E6, Emin7, E13). The most widely used description is followed by commonly used alternatives.

△ = major seventh
∅ = half diminished
o = diminished

6 HARMONIC SPELLING The harmonic spelling of each chord is given numerically (1 - 3 - 5), and in note names (E - G# - B). This provides extra reference material for more advanced players. If you are just beginning, feel free to ignore it!

7 FINGERBOARD LOCATION A number below the first fret of the chord box indicates which section of the guitar fingerboard the box relates to—"1" indicates first fret and higher numbers indicate the chord is played higher up the neck.

8 CHORD PHOTOGRAPH A photograph of the chord encourages correct fretting technique and shows what to do with fingers not introduced in the chord. Both acoustic and electric guitars are shown, as this book applies to both.

Chord symbols

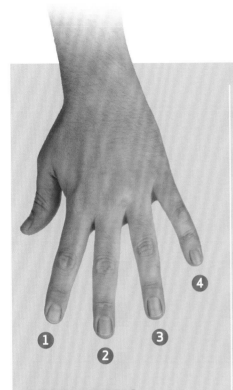

❌ Open string not sounded in chord.

◉ Open string sounded in chord.

▣ Open string root note sounded in chord (e.g. an E note in an E chord).

1 Indicates fingerboard finger positioning (the number indicates which finger should be used) and also that the fretted note is a root note.

① Indicates fingerboard finger positioning where the note is not the root note of the chord.

①①① A line crossing two or more strings denotes a barre, where two or more strings are fretted simultaneously with one finger.

(2) Alternative fingerings are occasionally provided next to the blue and red symbols. These are sometimes preferable for a quicker change to a particular chord shape.

FINGER NUMBERS
Standard hand fingering has been used throughout.

Anatomy of the guitar

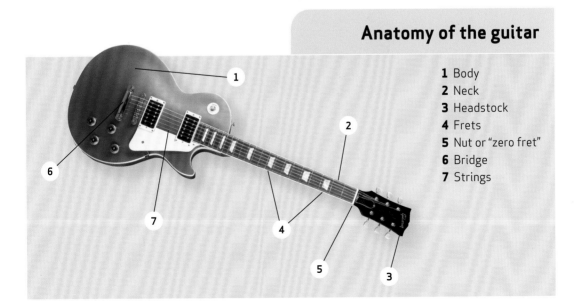

1 Body
2 Neck
3 Headstock
4 Frets
5 Nut or "zero fret"
6 Bridge
7 Strings

THE FINGERBOARD

Finding notes on the fingerboard is not easy; even accomplished players can be sketchy on this knowledge if they have learnt primarily "by ear." This easy-to-use diagram is intended to help you locate any note on the fingerboard—fast! Remember that after the twelfth fret the entire fingerboard repeats an octave higher (starting with the open string note name).

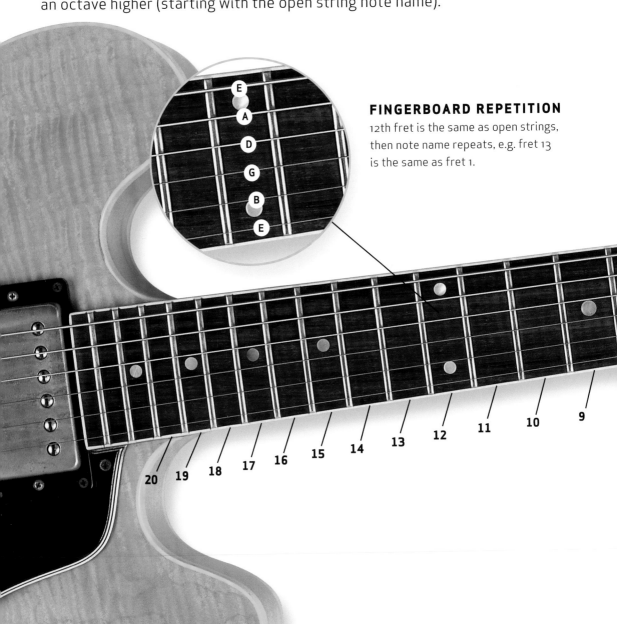

FINGERBOARD REPETITION
12th fret is the same as open strings, then note name repeats, e.g. fret 13 is the same as fret 1.

FRET 1

6 - F
5 - A#/Bb
4 - D#/Eb
3 - G#/Ab
2 - C
1 - F

FRET 2

6 - F#/Gb
5 - B
4 - E
3 - A
2 - C#
1 - F#/Gb

FRET 3

6 - G
5 - C
4 - F
3 - A#/Bb
2 - D
1 - G

FRET 4

6 - G#/Ab
5 - C#/Db
4 - F#/Gb
3 - B
2 - D#/Eb
1 - G#/Ab

FRET 5

6 - A
5 - D
4 - G
3 - C
2 - E
1 - A

FRET 6

6 - A#/Bb
5 - D#/Eb
4 - G#/Ab
3 - C#/Db
2 - F
1 - A#/Bb

FRET 7

6 - B
5 - E
4 - A
3 - D
2 - F#
1 - B

FRET 8

6 - C
5 - F
4 - A#/Bb
3 - D#/Eb
2 - G
1 - C

FRET 9

6 - C#/Db
5 - F#/Gb
4 - B
3 - E
2 - G#/Ab
1 - C#/Db

FRET 10

6 - D
5 - G
4 - C
3 - F
2 - A
1 - D

FRET 11

6 - D#/Eb
5 - G#/Ab
4 - C#/Db
3 - F#/Gb
2 - A#/Bb
1 - D#/Eb

FRET 12

6 - E
5 - A
4 - D
3 - G
2 - B
1 - E

OPEN STRINGS

When a string is included in a chord without being fretted it is called an "open string."

CHORD DIRECTORY

C

C MAJOR

C major is an important key since it is the starting point from which all other keys are derived. On the keyboard a C major scale is the easiest scale to play since it comprises only white keys or "natural" notes. **1** A favorite chord for beginners and a full-sounding resonant voicing that features in many famous songs and riffs. **3** A first inversion of C with its third (E) as the lowest note.

1 C (Cmaj, Cmajor, CM)

1 - 3 - 5
C - E - G

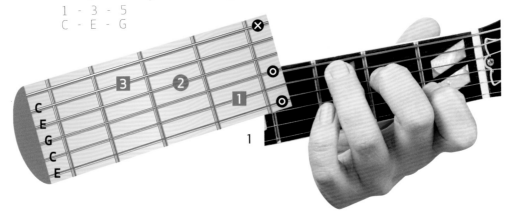

2 C (Cmaj, Cmajor, CM)

1 - 3 - 5
C - E - G

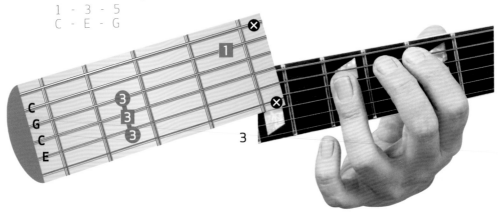

3   C (Cmaj, Cmajor, CM)

1 - 3 - 5
C - E - G

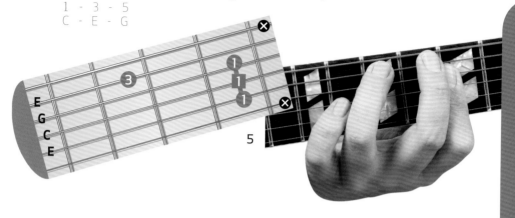

E
G
C
C
E

5

4   C (Cmaj, Cmajor, CM)

1 - 3 - 5
C - E - G

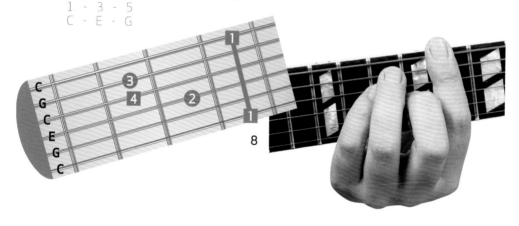

C
C
C
E
G
C

8

5   C (Cmaj, Cmajor, CM)

1 - 3 - 5
C - E - G

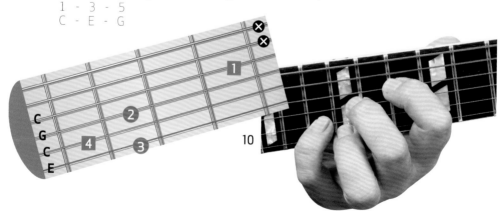

C
G
C
E

10

C MAJOR

A classic "ending" chord that's been used by everyone from Louis Armstrong to The Beatles, the sixth can also be used as a substitute for a basic major chord. **2** A resonant five-string chord with a doubled root (C) that's perfect for endings. **5** High-register, four-string voicing great for creating choppy, syncopated rhythm parts.

1 ## C6 (Cmaj6, Cmajor6, CM6)

1 - 3 - 5 - 6
C - E - G - A

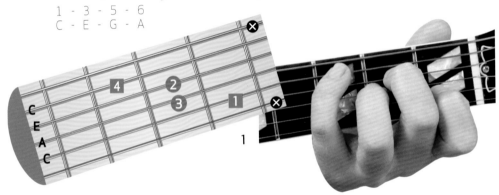

2 ## C6 (Cmaj6, Cmajor6, CM6)

1 - 3 - 5 - 6
C - E - G - A

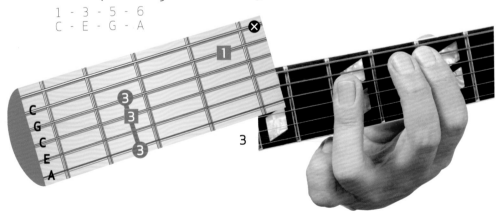

3 ## C6 (Cmaj6, Cmajor6, CM6)

1 - 3 - 5 - 6
C - E - G - A

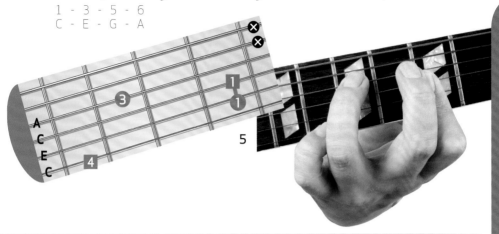

C

---

4 ## C6 (Cmaj6, Cmajor6, CM6)

1 - 3 - 5 - 6
C - E - G - A

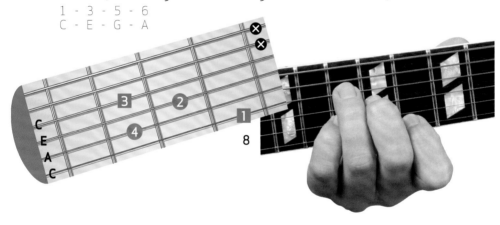

---

5 ## C6 (Cmaj6, Cmajor6, CM6)

1 - 3 - 5 - 6
C - E - G - A

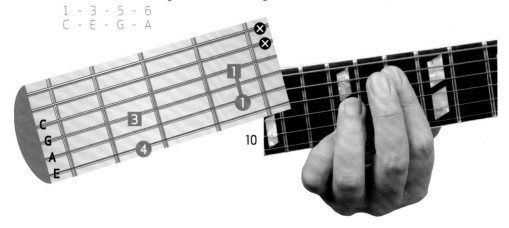

C

C MAJOR

The jazziest and coolest of all major chords, the major seventh chord isn't just for jazz—it features in plenty of rock songs too. **1** This wonderfully jangly, open major seventh voicing is great for strummed acoustic guitar work. **4** A popular jazz voicing that also works well when used in strummed rhythm parts.

1 ## Cmaj7 (C△, Cmajor7, CM7)

1 - 3 - 5 - 7
C - E - G - B

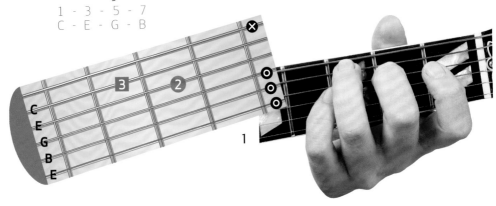

2 ## Cmaj7 (C△, Cmajor7, CM7)

1 - 3 - 5 - 7
C - E - G - B

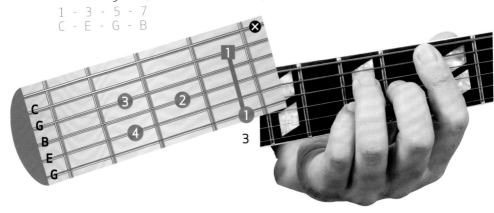

3

Cmaj7 (C△, Cmajor7, CM7)

1 - 3 - 5 - 7
C - E - G - B

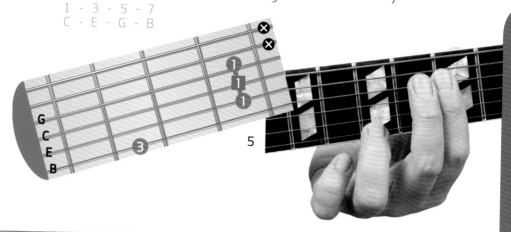

4

Cmaj7 (C△, Cmajor7, CM7)

1 - 3 - 5 - 7
C - E - G - B

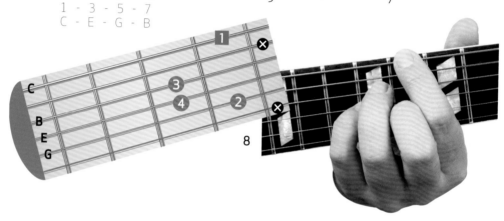

5

Cmaj7 (C△, Cmajor7, CM7)

1 - 3 - 5 - 7
C - E - G - B

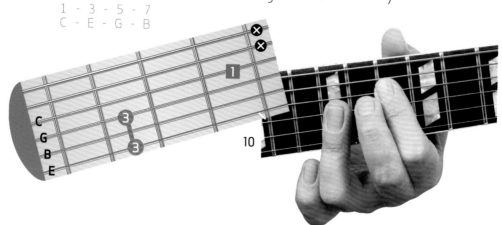

C MAJOR
Csus (C suspended)

Suspended chords "spice up" a chord sequence or static chord vamp and work well with similarly voiced major chords.
Csus4: 1 An open suspended chord with a doubled root (C).
Csus2: 2 The ubiquitous sus2 barre chord voicing, favored by many rock guitarists during the 1980s.

1 Csus4

1 - 4 - 5
C - F - G

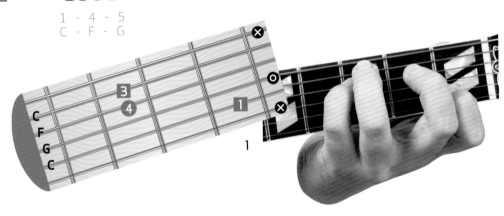

2 Csus4

1 - 4 - 5
C - F - G

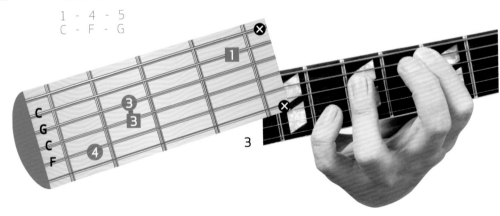

1 Csus2

1 - 2 - 5
C - D - G

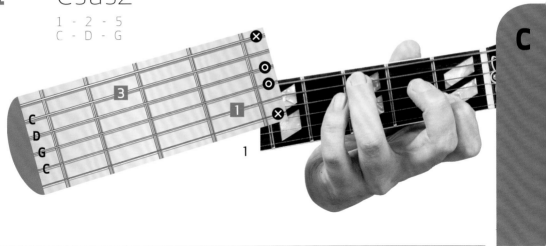

C

2 Csus2

1 - 2 - 5
C - D - G

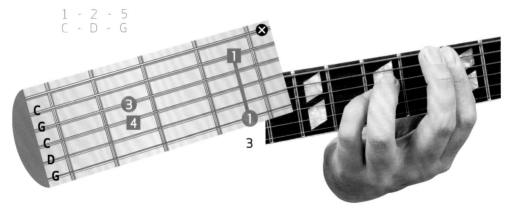

3 Csus2

1 - 2 - 5
C - D - G

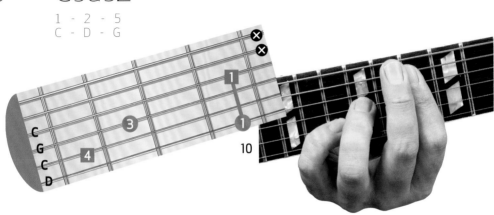

C MINOR

The relative minor of Eb major, C minor is a common key for minor blues progressions and is frequently used by many guitarists.
1 This tricky open shape is more prevalent in classical music, but sounds great played fingerstyle or arpeggiated with a pick.
4 Versatile full six-string barre played at the eighth fret.

1 ## Cm (Cmin, Cminor, C−)

1 - b3 - 5
C - Eb - G

2 ## Cm (Cmin, Cminor, C−)

1 - b3 - 5
C - Eb - G

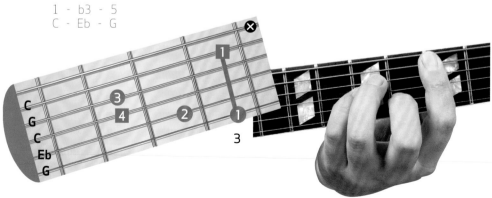

3 Cm (Cmin, Cminor, C−)

1 - b3 - 5
C - Eb - G

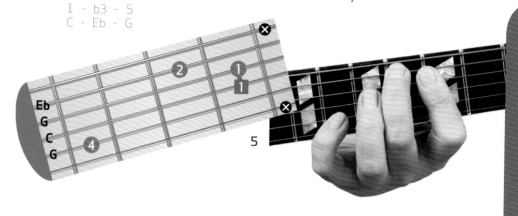

4 Cm (Cmin, Cminor, C−)

1 - b3 - 5
C - Eb - G

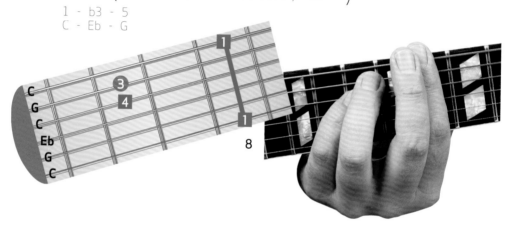

5 Cm (Cmin, Cminor, C−)

1 - b3 - 5
C - Eb - G

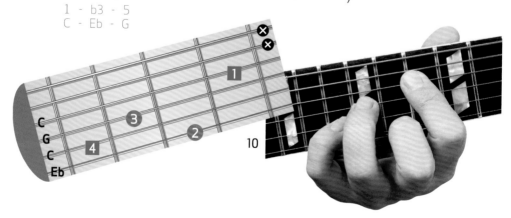

C

C MINOR

Minor sixth chords can be used as a substitute for a minor chord when more texture and color is required. Minor seventh chords are frequently used as static vamp chords (especially for funk and fusion) or to precede a dominant seventh whose root note is a fifth away (i.e. as the second chord in a II - V - I progression).

1 ## Cmin6 (Cminor6, Cm6, C−6)

1 - b3 - 5 - 6
C - Eb - G - A

2 ## Cmin6 (Cminor6, Cm6, C−6)

1 - b3 - 5 - 6
C - Eb - G - A

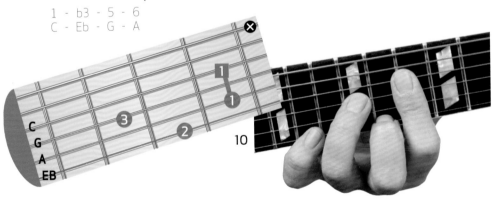

2 Cmin7 (Cminor7, Cm7, C−7)

1 - b3 - 5 - b7
C - Eb - G - Bb

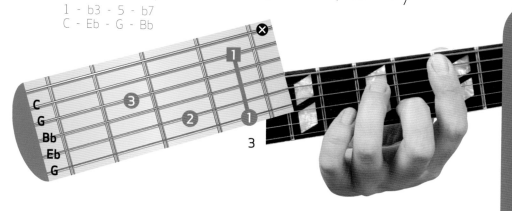

2 Cmin7 (Cminor7, Cm7, C−7)

1 - b3 - 5 - b7
C - Eb - G - Bb

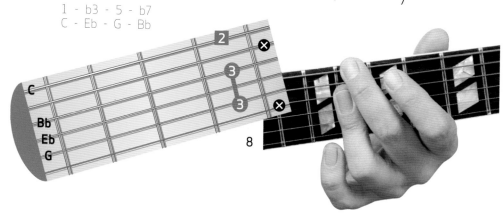

3 Cmin7 (Cminor7, Cm7, C−7)

1 - b3 - 5 - b7
C - Eb - G - Bb

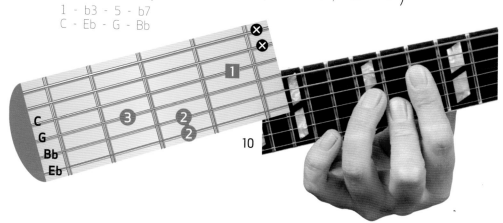

C7

C

No self-respecting blues guitarist should leave home without these five essential dominant seventh chords! **1** An open C7 voicing that is equally suited to fingerstyle or strummed rhythms. **3** High-register, four-string inversion with the fifth (G) as the lowest note—great for adding bite to a choppy rhythm guitar part.

1 ## C7 (Cdom7)

1 - 3 - 5 - b7
C - E - G - Bb

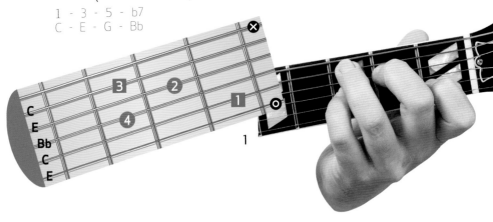

2 ## C7 (Cdom7)

1 - 3 - 5 - b7
C - E - G - Bb

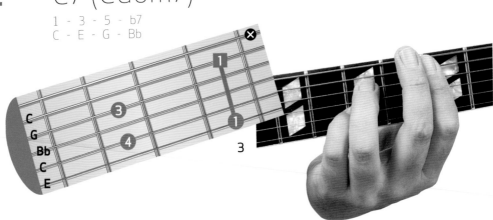

3   C7 (Cdom7)

1 - 3 - 5 - b7
C - E - G - Bb

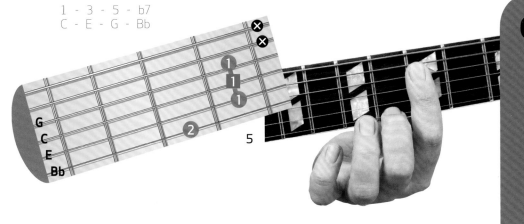

4   C7 (Cdom7)

1 - 3 - 5 - b7
C - E - G - Bb

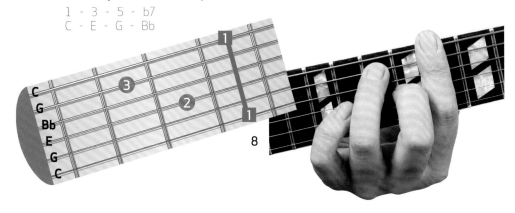

5   C7 (Cdom7)

1 - 3 - 5 - b7
C - E - G - Bb

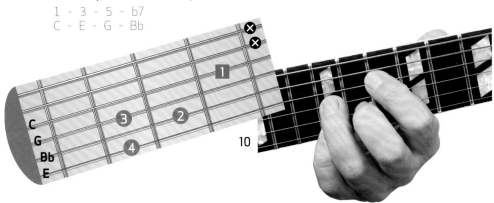

C7

C7#5 chords are "tension creating" dominant seventh chords and are most frequently used in a perfect cadence scenario, i.e. when a dominant chord (V) resolves to its tonic (I).
C7#5: 2 Try playing this chord followed by Fmaj7, shape 4 on page 109.
C7sus: 1 The C7sus chord creates less tension and has a more "open" sound and works well when paired with a similarly voiced C7 chord —e.g. this chord followed by C7, shape 2 on page 26.

---

1   ## C7#5 (C7aug, C7+)

1 - 3 - #5 - b7
C - E - G# - Bb

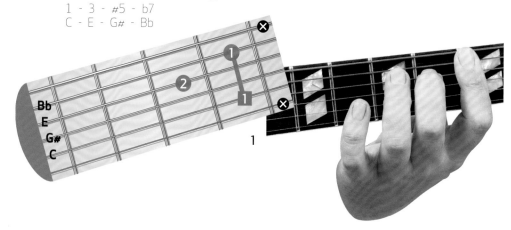

---

2   ## C7#5 (C7aug, C7+)

1 - 3 - #5 - b7
C - E - G# - Bb

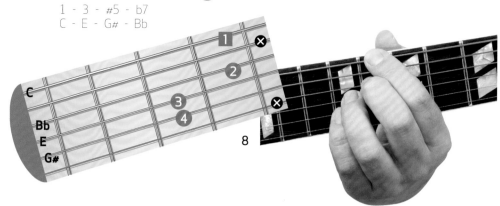

1

C7sus (C7sus4)

1 - 4 - 5 - b7
C - F - G - Bb

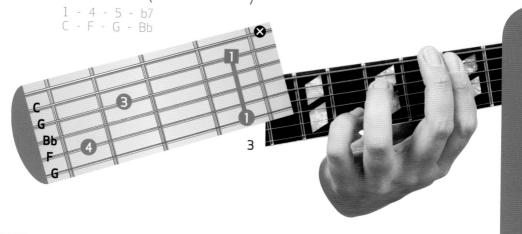

2

C7sus (C7sus4)

1 - 4 - 5 - b7
C - F - G - Bb

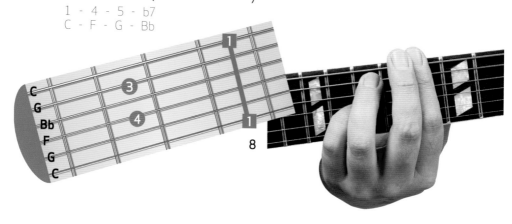

3

C7sus (C7sus4)

1 - 4 - 5 - b7
C - F - G - Bb

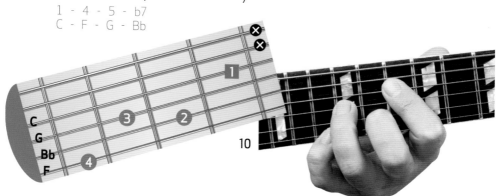

C

C7

A selection of dominant sevenths with various "color tensions" added to create harmonic interest.

C7#9 This is often referred to as the "Hendrix chord" since Jimi frequently used #9 chords in his compositions.

C13: 1 and 2 These chords are not only great for jazzers—they are also used in funk and all related dance styles.

- ## C9 (Cdom9)

1 - 3 - 5 - b7 - 9
C - E - G - Bb - D

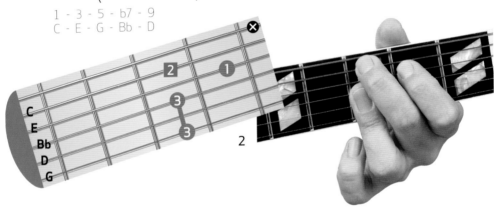

- ## C7#9

1 - 3 - 5 - b7 - #9
C - E - G - Bb - D#

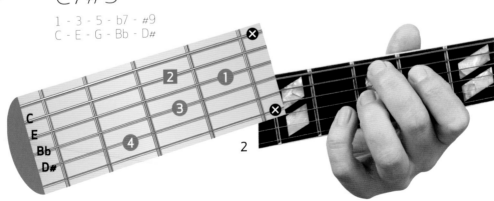

● C7b9

1 - 3 - 5 - b7 - b9
C - E - G - Bb - Db

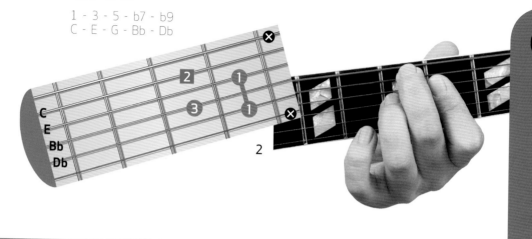

1 C13

1 - 3 - 5 - b7 - 9 - 13
C - E - G - Bb - D - A

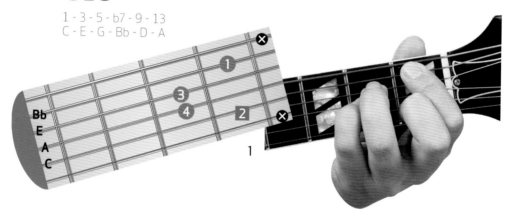

2 C13

1 - 3 - 5 - b7 - 9 - 13
C - E - G - Bb - D - A

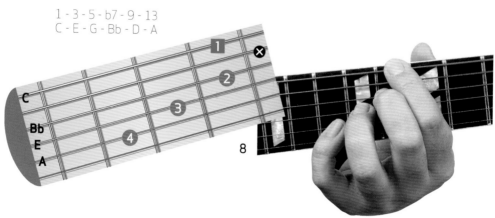

C#

C#/Db MAJOR

C# major is an infrequently used key due to the key signature containing no less than seven sharps (every scale note is sharpened). This makes it an unpopular key for sightreading.
1 A four-string inversion with the third (E#) as the lowest note.
5 Another four-string chord, this is a high-register, root position voicing—great for second guitar rhythm parts.

1 C# (C#maj, C#major, C#M)

1 - 3 - 5
C# - E# - G#

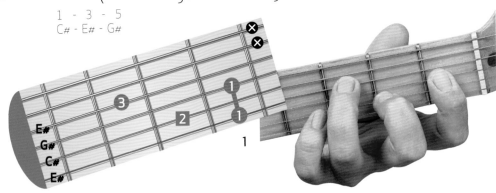

2 C# (C#maj, C#major, C#M)

1 - 3 - 5
C# - E# - G#

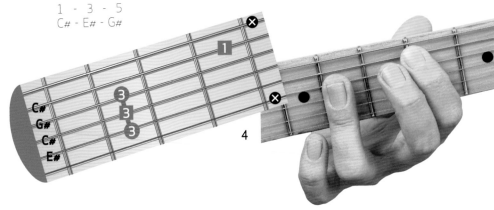

3 C# (C#maj, C#major, C#M)

1 - 3 - 5
C# - E# - G#

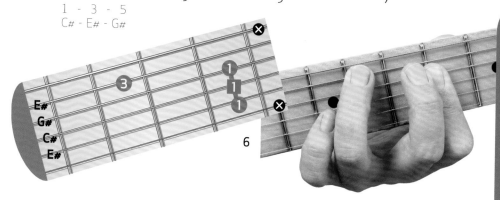

4 C# (C#maj, C#major, C#M)

1 - 3 - 5
C# - E# - G#

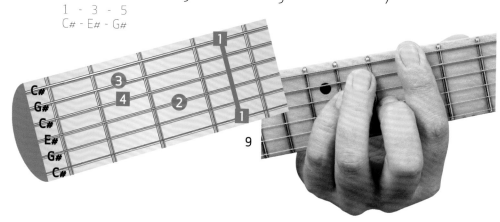

5 C# (C#maj, C#major, C#M)

1 - 3 - 5
C# - E# - G#

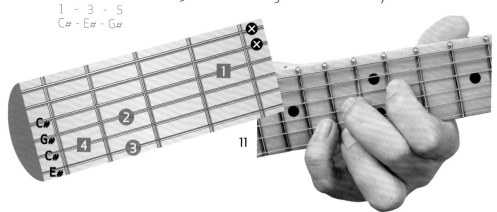

C#/Db MAJOR

Sixth chords are so called because they add the interval of a sixth to the basic major triad, hence the 1 - 3 - 5 - 6 harmonic spelling of these chords. **1** Warm and jazzy, four-string voicing with muted outer strings. **4** This four-string sixth voicing is ideally suited for blues rhythm guitar.

1 C#6 (C#maj6, C#major6, C#M6)

1 - 3 - 5 - 6
C# - E# - G# - A#

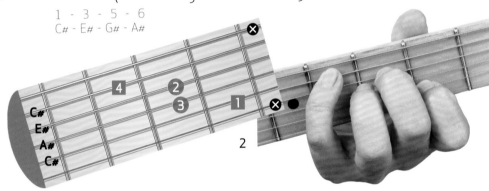

2 C#6 (C#maj6, C#major6, C#M6)

1 - 3 - 5 - 6
C# - E# - G# - A#

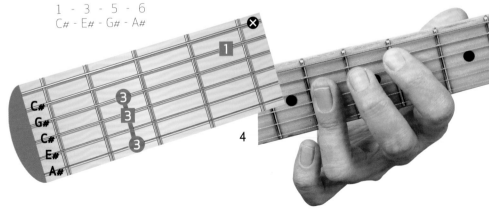

3 C#6 (C#maj6, C#major6, C#M6)

1 - 3 - 5 - 6
C# - E# - G# - A#

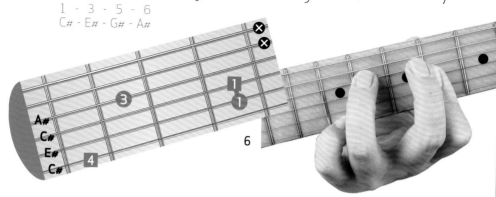

4 C#6 (C#maj6, C#major6, C#M6)

1 - 3 - 5 - 6
C# - E# - G# - A#

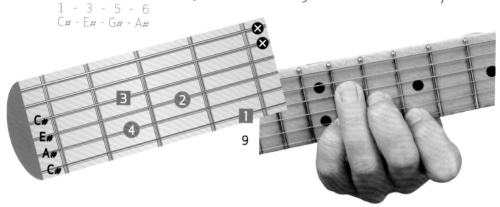

5 C#6 (C#maj6, C#major6, C#M6)

1 - 3 - 5 - 6
C# - E# - G# - A#

C#/Db MAJOR

The smooth-sounding major seventh chord can be used in many musical situations; from sweet jazz comps to distorted rock jangle, this chord will add color to any progression.
1 A big stretch is required for the lowest C#maj7 on the neck. Try omitting the fourth finger if you find it tricky.
5 This chiming, four-string major seventh chord can sweeten any chord progression.

---

1 C#maj7 (C#Δ, C#major7, C#M7)
1 - 3 - 5 - 7
C# - E# - G# - B#

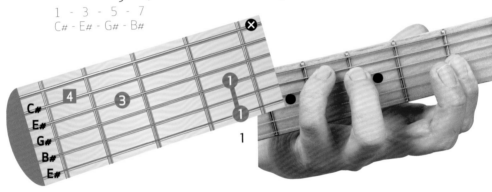

---

2 C#maj7 (C#Δ, C#major7, C#M7)
1 - 3 - 5 - 7
C# - E# - G# - B#

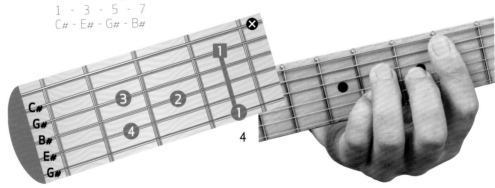

3 C#maj7 (C#△, C#major7, C#M7)

1 - 3 - 5 - 7
C# - E# - G# - B#

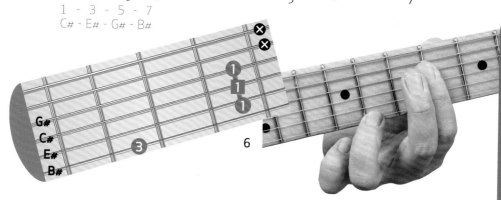

4 C#maj7 (C#△, C#major7, C#M7)

1 - 3 - 5 - 7
C# - E# - G# - B#

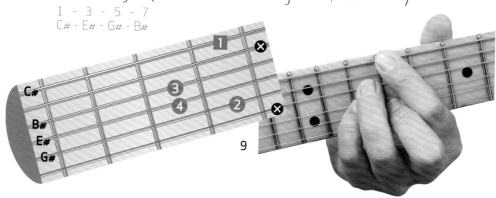

5 C#maj7 (C#△, C#major7, C#M7)

1 - 3 - 5 - 7
C# - E# - G# - B#

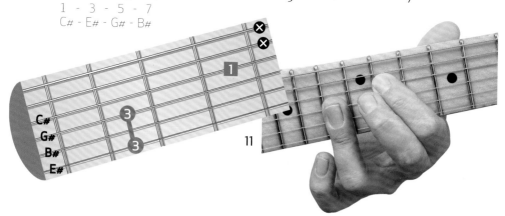

C#/DbMAJOR
C#sus (C# suspended)

Suspended chords are often used to create harmonic ambiguity since they contain no third and are neither major nor minor.

C#sus2: 2 A high four-string voicing that's great for biting rhythm parts.

C#sus4: 2 Create a big sound with this six-string sus4 voicing—this works well when mixed with C# major, shape 4 on page 33.

1 C#sus2

1 - 2 - 5
C# - D# - G#

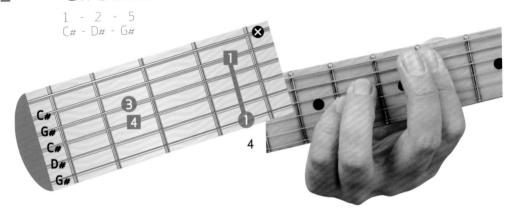

2 C#sus2

1 - 2 - 5
C# - D# - G#

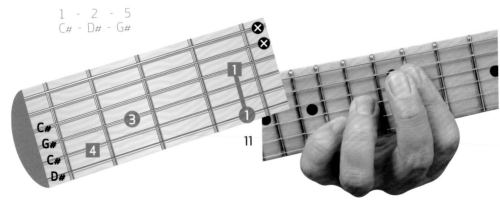

1

C#sus4

1 - 4 - 5
C# - F# - G#

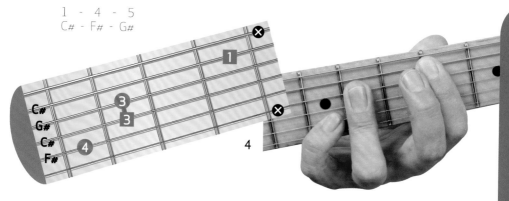

2

C#sus4

1 - 4 - 5
C# - F# - G#

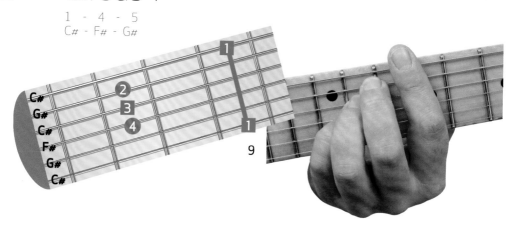

3

C#sus4

1 - 4 - 5
C# - F# - G#

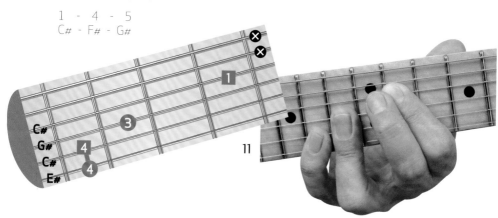

C#

C#/Db MINOR

The key of C# minor (which contains four sharps) is the relative key of E major (a very common guitar key) and is frequently encountered. **1** This shape requires a big stretch between the third and fourth fingers —if you find this difficult, omit the top note. **3** A four-string inversion played on the inner strings with the minor third as the lowest note.

1 ## C#m (C#min, C#minor, C#—)

1 - b3 - 5
C# - E - G#

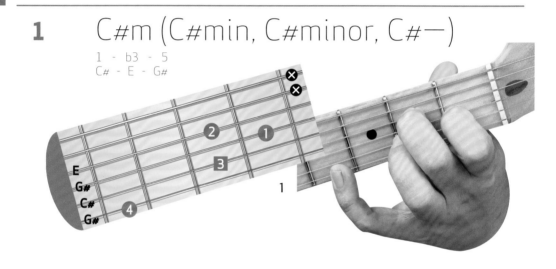

2 ## C#m (C#min, C#minor, C#—)

1 - b3 - 5
C# - E - G#

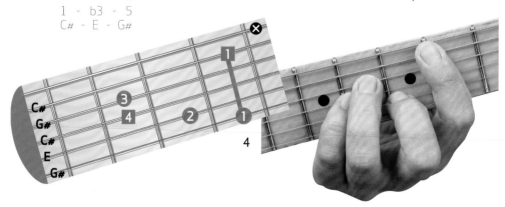

3

C#m (C#min, C#minor, C#−)

1 - b3 - 5
C# - E - G#

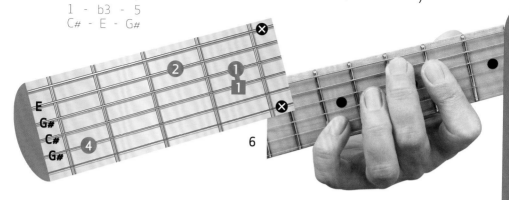

4

C#m (C#min, C#minor, C#−)

1 - b3 - 5
C# - E - G#

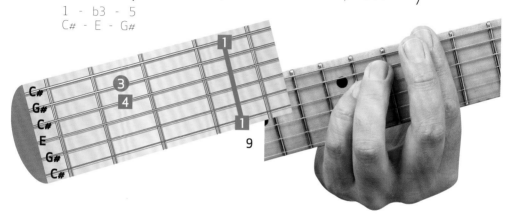

5

C#m (C#min, C#minor, C#−)

1 - b3 - 5
C# - E - G#

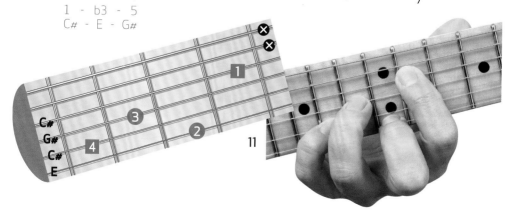

C#/Db MINOR

Adding the sixth or the flattened seventh is a great way to introduce some color to a basic minor chord.

C#min6: 1 This resonant chord has its root played separately on the sixth string—notice that the first and fifth strings should be muted.

C#min7: 1 Versatile minor seventh voicing with a doubled 5th (G#).

1   C#min6 (C#minor6, C#m6, C#−6)

1 - b3 - 5 - 6
C# - E - G# - A#

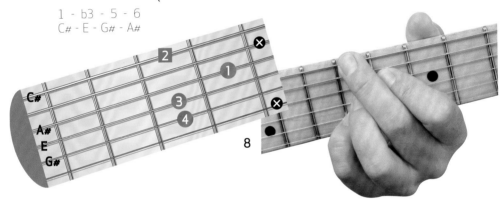

2   C#min6 (C#minor6, C#m6, C#−6)

1 - b3 - 5 - 6
C# - E - G# - A#

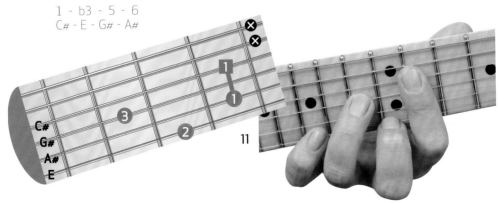

1 C#min7 (C#minor7, C#m7, C#—7)

1 - b3 - 5 - b7
C# - E - G# - B

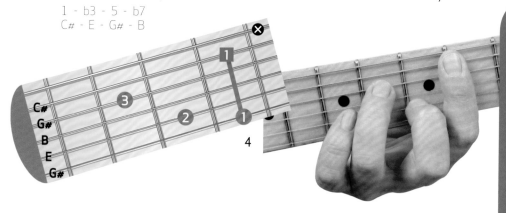

2 C#min7 (C#minor7, C#m7, C#—7)

1 - b3 - 5 - b7
C# - E - G# - B

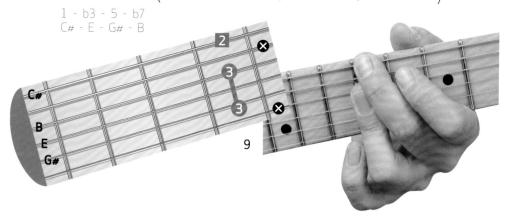

3 C#min7 (C#minor7, C#m7, C#—7)

1 - b3 - 5 - b7
C# - E - G# - B

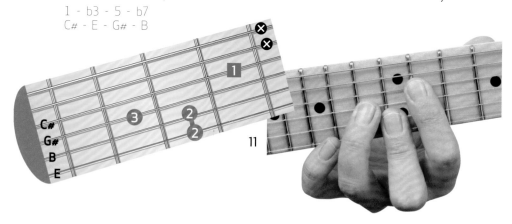

C#7/Db7

A dominant seventh can be used as a static chord (e.g. the first chord of a blues), or as a "going home" cadence chord. C#7 can resolve to either F# major or F# minor. **1** This four-note seventh voicing is a favorite among fingerstyle guitarists who often add the low fifth (G#) on the sixth string to create an alternating bassline.

1 C#7 (C#dom7)

1 - 3 - 5 - b7
C# - E - G# - B

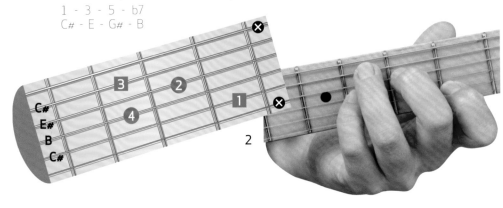

2 C#7 (C#dom7)

1 - 3 - 5 - b7
C# - E - G# - B

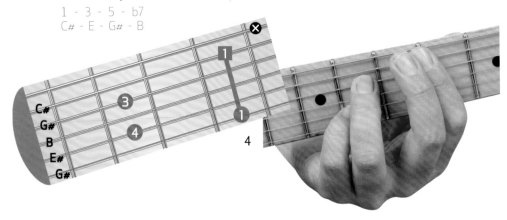

3 C#7 (C#dom7)

1 - 3 - 5 - b7
C# - E - G# - B

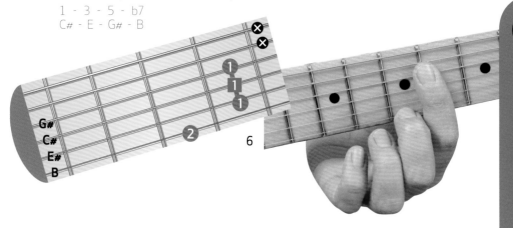

4 C#7 (C#dom7)

1 - 3 - 5 - b7
C# - E - G# - B

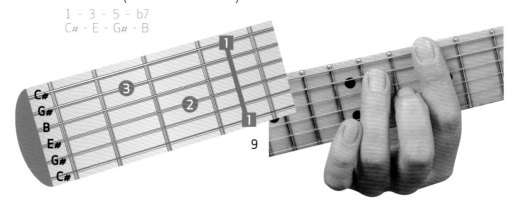

5 C#7 (C#dom7)

1 - 3 - 5 - b7
C# - E - G# - B

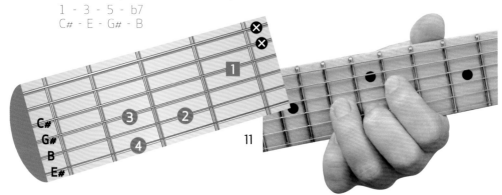

C#7/Db7

C#

Adding a sharpened fifth to a dominant seventh chord creates tension and heightens the "pull" back to the home chord in a perfect (V–I) cadence.
C#7#5: 1 Dark and moody inversion with the flattened seventh (B) in the bass.
C#7sus: 3 High-register, four-string suspended seventh—ideal for syncopated rhythm work—create syncopations by "choking" the chord (releasing the pressure of your fretting hand).

1 C#7#5 (C#7aug, C#7+)

1 - 3 - #5 - b7
C# - E# - G## - B

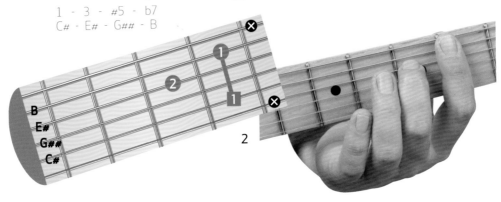

2 C#7#5 (C#7aug, C#7+)

1 - 3 - #5 - b7
C# - E# - G## - B

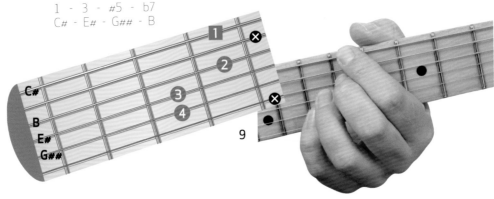

3 C#7sus (C#7sus4)

1 - 4 - 5 - b7
C# - F# - G# - B

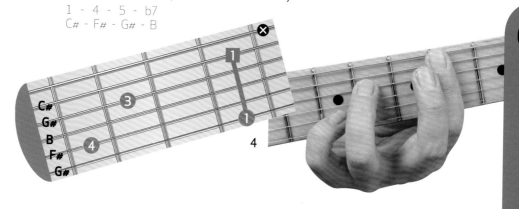

4 C#7sus (C#7sus4)

1 - 4 - 5 - b7
C# - F# - G# - B

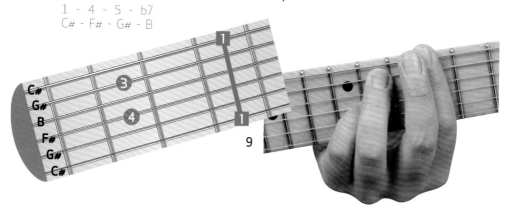

5 C#7sus (C#7sus4)

1 - 4 - 5 - b7
C# - F# - G# - B

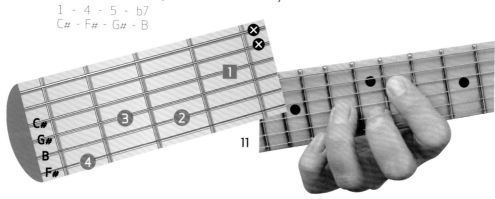

C#7/Db7

Ninths create additional harmonic interest when added to a dominant seventh. Altered ninth voicings (#9/b9) create tension and heighten the resolution when used in a perfect (V–1) cadence; natural ninth chords are frequently used as a static vamp chord in blues and funk tunes. The jazzy thirteenth is a very versatile chord and is used in many genres.

• C#9 (C#dom9)

1 - 3 - 5 - b7 - 9
C# - E# - G# - B - D#

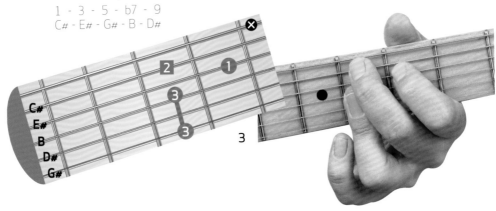

• C#7#9

1 - 3 - 5 - b7 - #9
C# - E# - G# - B - D##

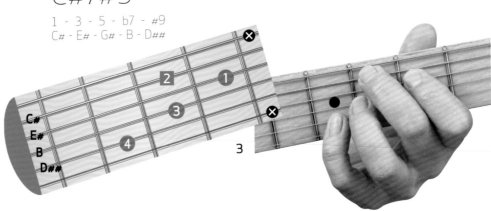

- ## C#7b9

1 - 3 - 5 - b7 - b9
C# - E# - G# - B - D

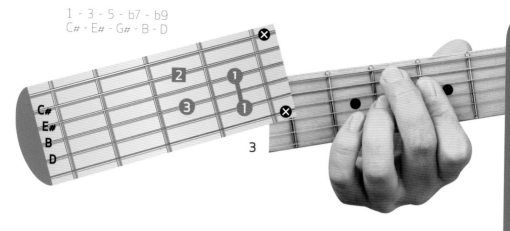

1 C#13

1 - 3 - 5 - b7 - 9 - 13
C# - E# - G# - B - D# - A#

2 C#13

1 - 3 - 5 - b7 - 9 - 13
C# - E# - G# - B - D# - A#

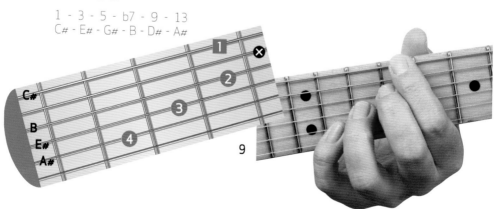

D MAJOR

D major is very "guitar-friendly" and many classic songs have been written in this key. **1** Basic resonant, open four-string chord that's ideal for strummed rhythm work. **2** A subtle variation of the previous chord, this four-string inversion has its third (F#) in the bass and is more suited to "choked" rhythm work since it can be easily damped.

1 ## D (Dmaj, Dmajor, DM)

1 - 3 - 5
D - F# - A

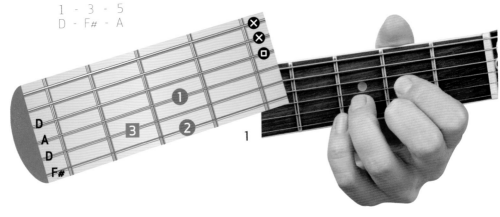

2 ## D (Dmaj, Dmajor, DM)

1 - 3 - 5
D - F# - A

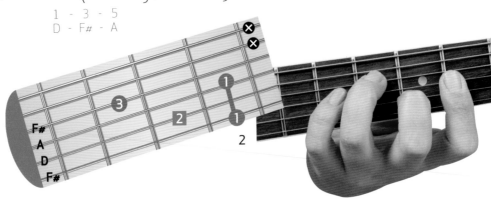

3

D (Dmaj, Dmajor, DM)

1 - 3 - 5
D - F# - A

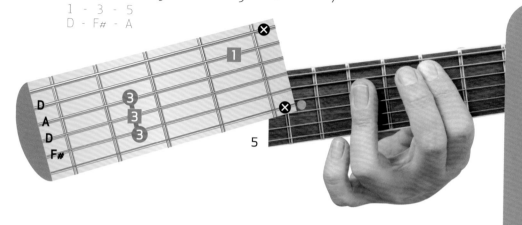

D

4

D (Dmaj, Dmajor, DM)

1 - 3 - 5
D - F# - A

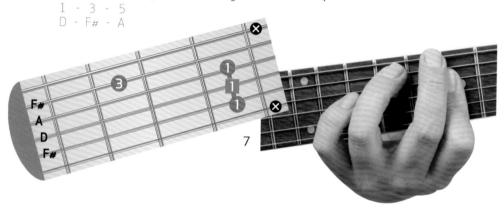

5

D (Dmaj, Dmajor, DM)

1 - 3 - 5
D - F# - A

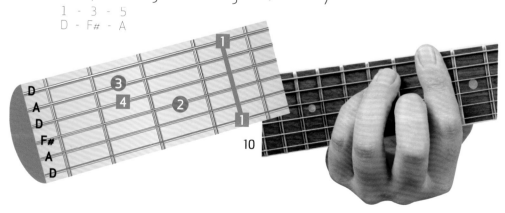

D MAJOR

The sixth chord should be your first choice when choosing a substitute for a basic major chord—the sixth interval will not clash with a tonic melody note (unlike the seventh in a major seventh chord). **1** Since it contains two open strings, this four-string sixth chord creates bright, jangling tones. **2** In contrast to the previous chord, this voicing has a warmer, jazzier sound.

1 ## D6 (Dmaj6, Dmajor6, DM6)

1 - 3 - 5 - 6
D - F# - A - B

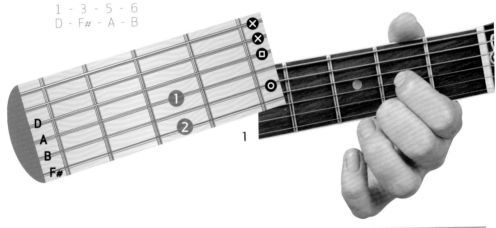

2 ## D6 (Dmaj6, Dmajor6, DM6)

1 - 3 - 5 - 6
D - F# - A - B

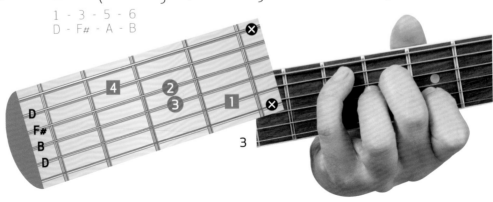

3

D6 (Dmaj6, Dmajor6, DM6)

1 - 3 - 5 - 6
D - F# - A - B

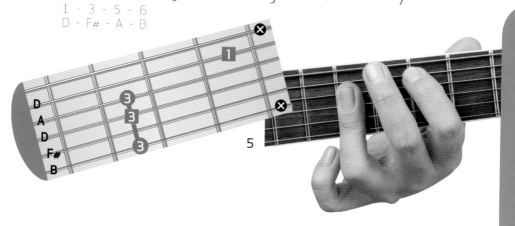

4

D6 (Dmaj6, Dmajor6, DM6)

1 - 3 - 5 - 6
D - F# - A - B

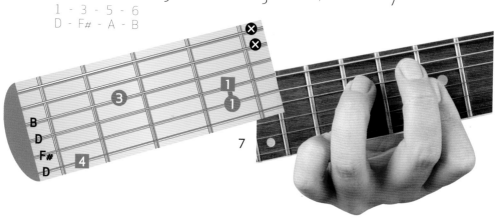

5

D6 (Dmaj6, Dmajor6, DM6)

1 - 3 - 5 - 6
D - F# - A - B

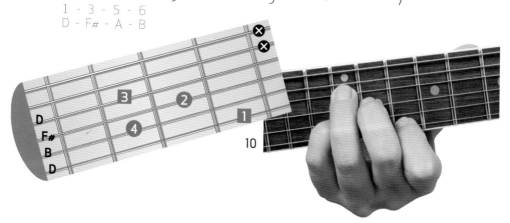

D

D MAJOR

The major seventh chord is often ignored by rock guitarists because of its jazzy connotations, but many of rock's pioneers (including Jimi Hendrix, Jeff Beck, and Jimmy Page) frequently incorporated this bright and breezy sounding chord in their work. **1** Open chords possess a resonant quality that other chords just don't have and this four-string major seventh is no exception.

1

Dmaj7 (D△, Dmajor7, DM7)

1 - 3 - 5 - 7
D - F# - A - C#

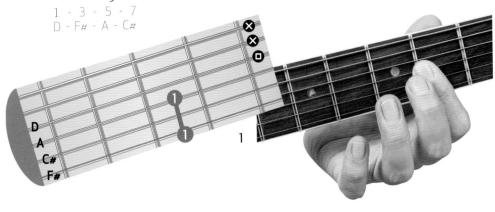

2

Dmaj7 (D△, Dmajor7, DM7)

1 - 3 - 5 - 7
D - F# - A - C#

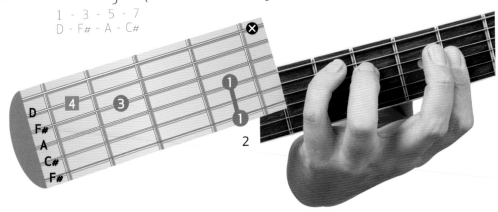

3 Dmaj7 (D△, Dmajor7, DM7)
1 - 3 - 5 - 7
D - F# - A - C#

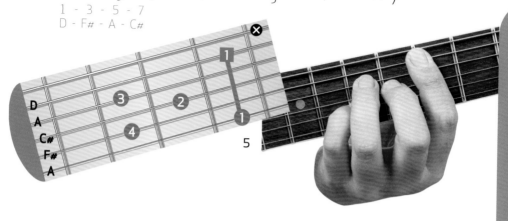

D

4 Dmaj7 (D△, Dmajor7, DM7)
1 - 3 - 5 - 7
D - F# - A - C#

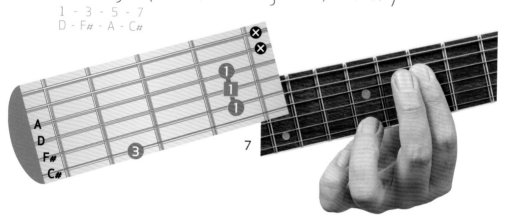

5 Dmaj7 (D△, Dmajor7, DM7)
1 - 3 - 5 - 7
D - F# - A - C#

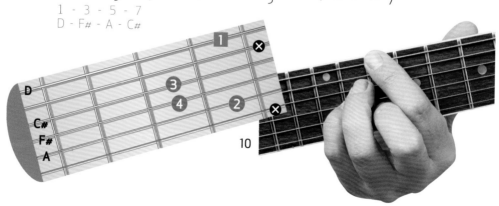

D MAJOR
Dsus (D suspended)

A suspended chord temporarily "suspends" the third of a chord by replacing it with the second or the fourth—this can then be resolved by reverting to the major chord, or simply be left "hanging" to intensify the harmonic tension.

Dsus2: 1 With two of the notes in this four-string shape on open strings, this chord will produce a full, resonant sound.

1 ## Dsus2
1 - 2 - 5
D - E - A

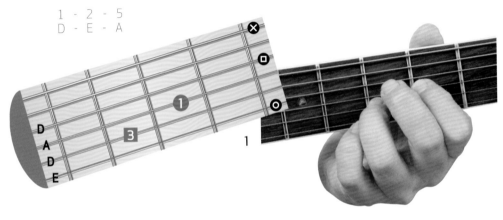

2 ## Dsus2
1 - 2 - 5
D - E - A

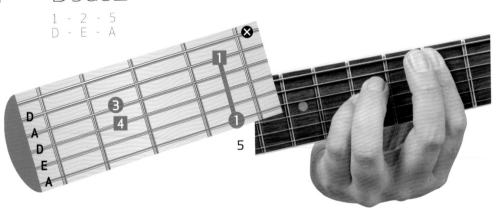

D

1 Dsus4
1 - 4 - 5
D - G - A

1

2 Dsus4
1 - 4 - 5
D - G - A

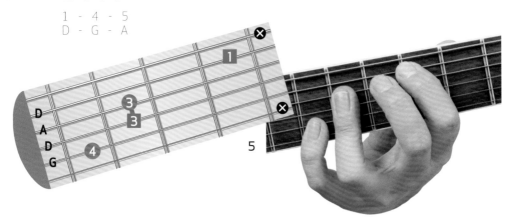

5

3 Dsus4
1 - 4 - 5
D - G - A

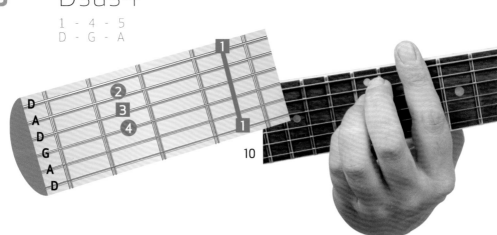

10

D

D MINOR

Immortalized in the classic rockumentary spoof *This is Spinal Tap*
as "the saddest of all keys," D minor is a very popular guitar key.
1 A simple, open four-string chord that has a dark, almost medieval quality.
3 This versatile five-string barre chord was most famously used in Pink
Floyd's "Another Brick In The Wall" to create a hypnotic, choked, rhythm
guitar riff.

1 Dm (Dmin, Dminor, D−)

1 - b3 - 5
D - F - A

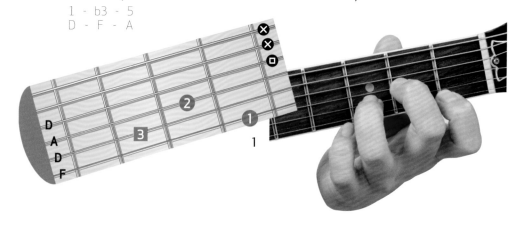

2 Dm (Dmin, Dminor, D−)

1 - b3 - 5
D - F - A

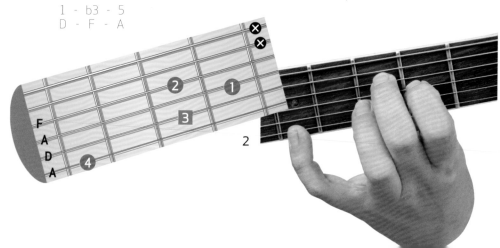

3   # Dm (Dmin, Dminor, D−)

1 - b3 - 5
D - F - A

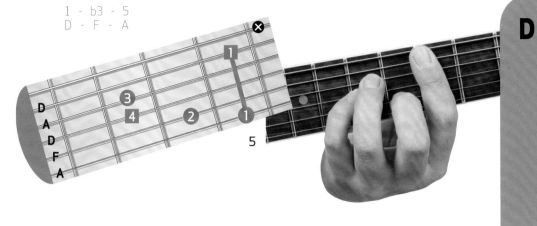

D

4   # Dm (Dmin, Dminor, D−)

1 - b3 - 5
D - F - A

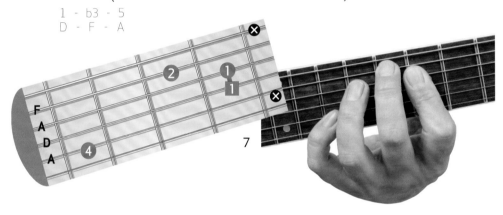

5   # Dm (Dmin, Dminor, D−)

1 - b3 - 5
D - F - A

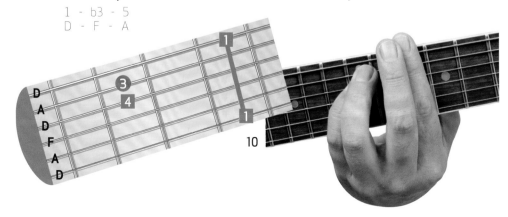

D

D MINOR

Don't be afraid to experiment with chord voicings—adding a sixth or a seventh to a basic minor chord will help you to create a more interesting accompaniment.

Dmin6: 1 This open minor six voicing is a dark and evocative chord that can be strummed with a pick, or fingerpicked for more atmospheric textures.

1
Dmin6 (Dminor6, Dm6, D–6)
1 - b3 - 5 - 6
D - F - A - B

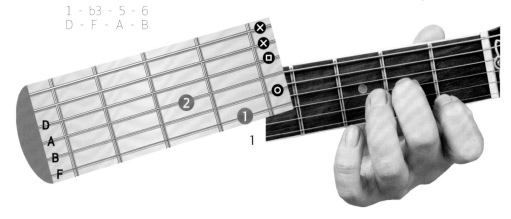

2
Dmin6 (Dminor6, Dm6, D–6)
1 - b3 - 5 - 6
D - F - A - B

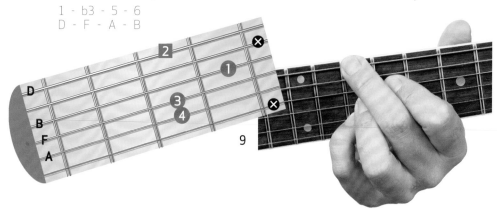

1 Dmin7 (Dminor7, Dm7, D−7)

1 - b3 - 5 - b7
D - F - A - C

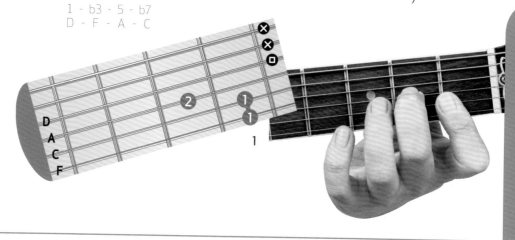

2 Dmin7 (Dminor7, Dm7, D−7)

1 - b3 - 5 - b7
D - F - A - C

3 Dmin7 (Dminor7, Dm7, D−7)

1 - b3 - 5 - b7
D - F - A - C

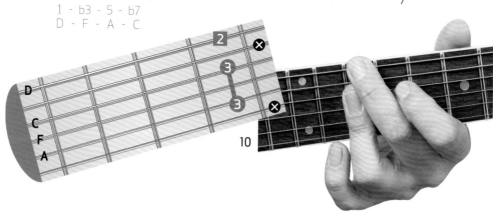

D

D 7

Dominant seventh chords have a characteristic quality that is used to create tension and motion. Their sound is derived from the interval of a flattened fifth between the b7 (C) and the 3rd (F#); this interval was actually banned during the Middle Ages since it was feared that playing it would summon Beelzebub! Hence the blues being named "the devil's music" with its dominant seventh based harmonies.

1

D7 (Ddom7)

1 - 3 - 5 - b7
D - F# - A - C

2

D7 (Ddom7)

1 - 3 - 5 - b7
D - F# - A - C

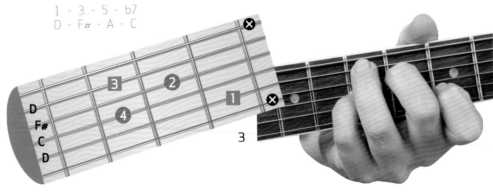

3 D7 (Ddom7)

1 - 3 - 5 - b7
D - F# - A - C

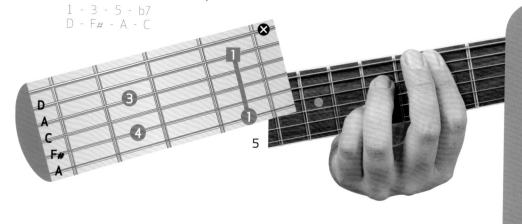

D

4 D7 (Ddom7)

1 - 3 - 5 - b7
D - F# - A - C

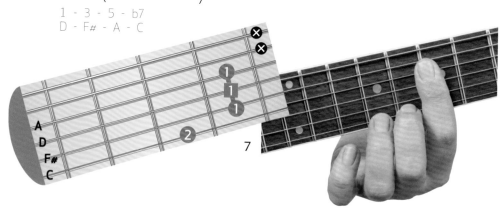

5 D7 (Ddom7)

1 - 3 - 5 - b7
D - F# - A - C

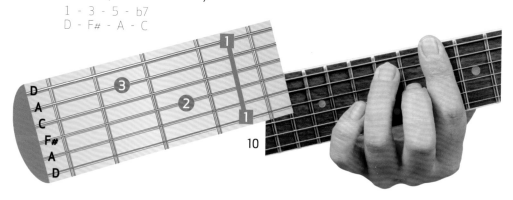

D

D7

Sharpening the fifth of a dominant seventh results in a much darker sounding chord that is often used to create extra tension when used in a V (D7) to I (G) scenario. Dominant sevenths with a suspended fourth create a less intense sense of anticipation—a famous example is the sustained 7sus4 chord that starts The Mamas And The Papas' 1960's classic "California Dreaming."

1 ## D7#5 (D7aug, D7+)

1 - 3 - #5 - b7
D - F# - A# - C

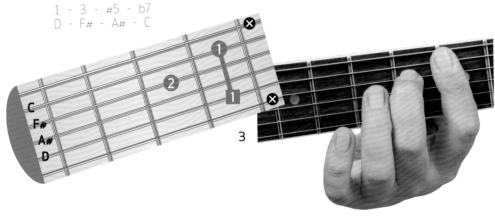

2 ## D7#5 (D7aug, D7+)

1 - 3 - #5 - b7
D - F# - A# - C

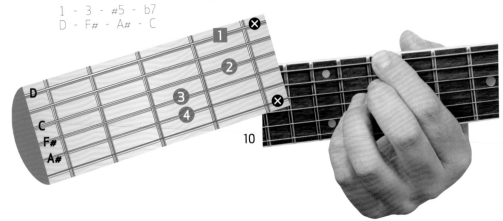

1   # D7sus (D7sus4)
1 - 4 - 5 - b7
D - G - A - C

D

2   # D7sus (D7sus4)
1 - 4 - 5 - b7
D - G - A - C

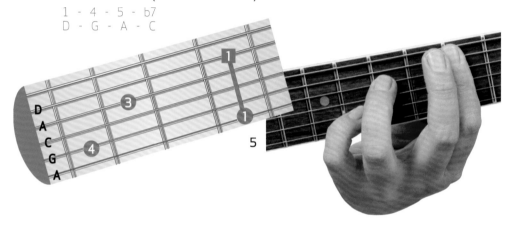

3   # D7sus (D7sus4)
1 - 4 - 5 - b7
D - G - A - C

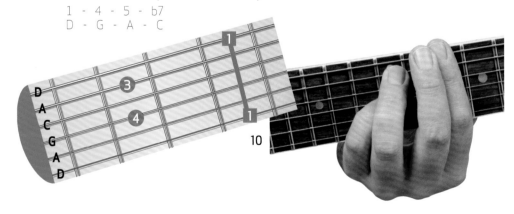

D 7

Ninth chords extend the dominant seventh by adding a ninth to the
chord. In guitar voicings, the fifth of the chord (A) is often omitted.
A thirteenth chord adds yet another interval to our ninth chord,
resulting in a six-note chord. To make the chord more playable,
thirteenth chords often omit the fifth (A) and the ninth (E).

D9 (Ddom9)

1 - 3 - 5 - b7 - 9
D - F# - A - C - E

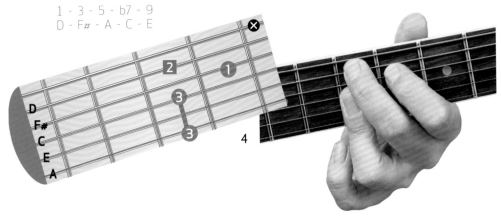

D7#9

1 - 3 - 5 - b7 - #9
D - F# - A - C - E#

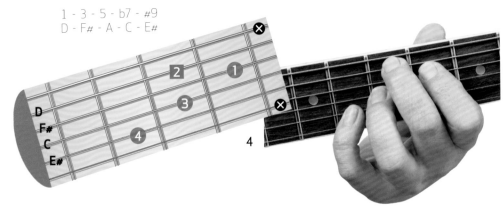

● ## D7b9
1 - 3 - 5 - b7 - b9
D - F# - A - C - Eb

1 ## D13
1 - 3 - 5 - b7 - 9 - 13
D - F# - A - C - E - B

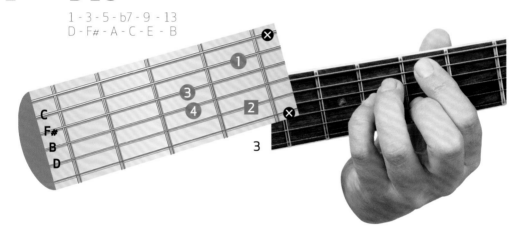

2 ## D13
1 - 3 - 5 - b7 - 9 - 13
D - F# - A - C - E - B

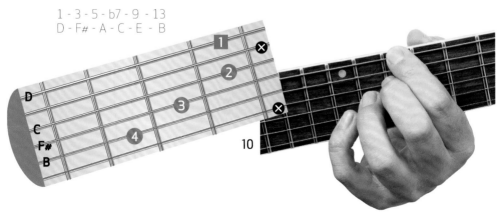

Eb/D# MAJOR

Since Eb is a great key for horn players (saxophone, trumpet, and trombone), any style of music that features these instruments (e.g. jazz, Chicago blues, soul, and funk) is more likely to favor this and other "flat" keys. **4** A useful four-string inversion and famously used in the intro of Jimi Hendrix's "The Wind Cries Mary" (Jimi actually extended the barre onto the fifth string so that he could "hammer-on" the lowest note).

1 Eb (Ebmaj, Ebmajor, EbM)

1 - 3 - 5
Eb - G - Bb

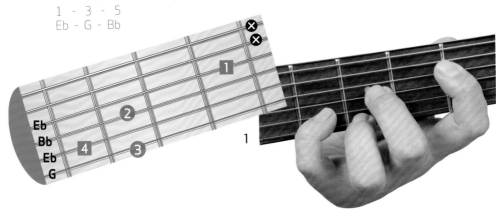

2 Eb (Ebmaj, Ebmajor, EbM)

1 - 3 - 5
Eb - G - Bb

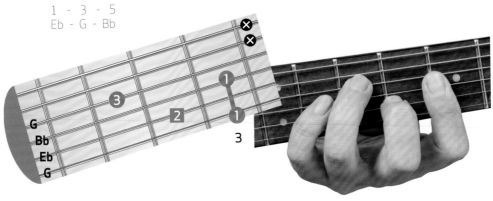

3 Eb (Ebmaj, Ebmajor, EbM)

1 - 3 - 5
Eb - G - Bb

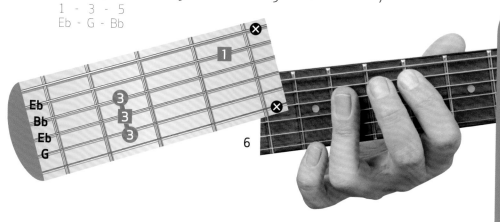

4 Eb (Ebmaj, Ebmajor, EbM)

1 - 3 - 5
Eb - G - Bb

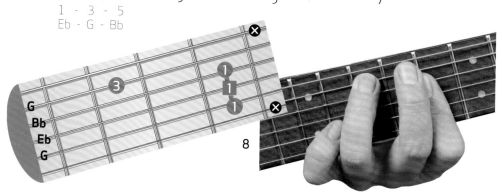

5 Eb (Ebmaj, Ebmajor, EbM)

1 - 3 - 5
Eb - G - Bb

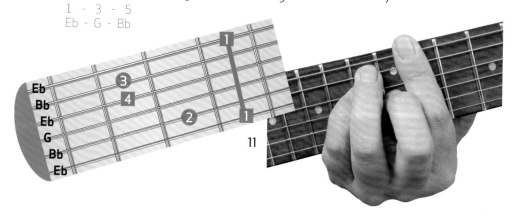

Eb/D# MAJOR

Adding a sixth to a major triad results in a four-note chord with more harmonic color than a basic major chord; it's the perfect way to add interest and a little "spice" to what might otherwise be a bland chord sequence.
4 A light and breezy sounding chord with the sixth (C) as its lowest note.

1 ## Eb6 (Ebmaj6, Ebmajor6, EbM6)

1 - 3 - 5 - 6
Eb - G - Bb - C

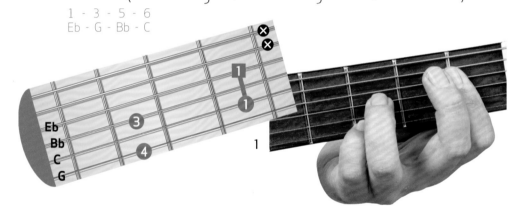

2 ## Eb6 (Ebmaj6, Ebmajor6, EbM6)

1 - 3 - 5 - 6
Eb - G - Bb - C

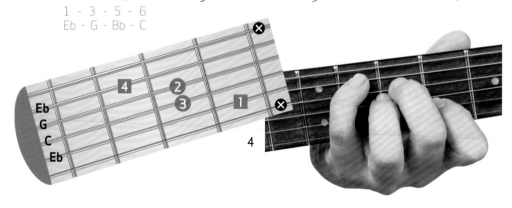

3   # Eb6 (Ebmaj6, Ebmajor6, EbM6)
1 - 3 - 5 - 6
Eb - G - Bb - C

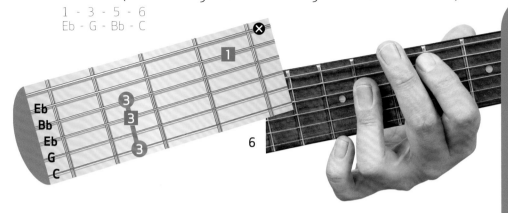

Eb

---

4   # Eb6 (Ebmaj6, Ebmajor6, EbM6)
1 - 3 - 5 - 6
Eb - G - Bb - C

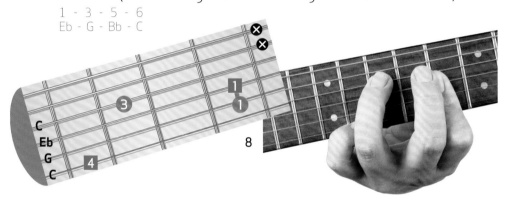

---

5   # Eb6 (Ebmaj6, Ebmajor6, EbM6)
1 - 3 - 5 - 6
Eb - G - Bb - C

Eb/D# MAJOR

Adding a major seventh interval to a major triad creates a chord that is somehow greater than the sum of its parts: mellow, floating, cool, and sophisticated. **3** An incredibly versatile five-string barre that sounds great just sustained, or which can be played staccato (by "choking" the chord with your fretting hand) to create syncopated rhythms.

1 Ebmaj7 (EbΔ, Ebmajor7, EbM7)

1 - 3 - 5 - 7
Eb - G - Bb - D

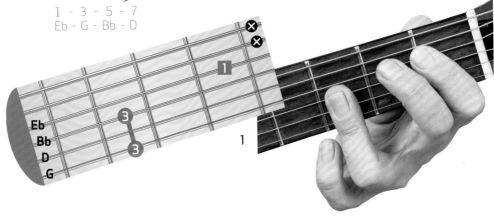

2 Ebmaj7 (EbΔ, Ebmajor7, EbM7)

1 - 3 - 5 - 7
Eb - G - Bb - D

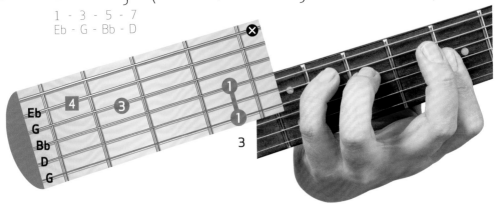

3 # Ebmaj7 (Eb△, Ebmajor7, EbM7)
1 - 3 - 5 - 7
Eb - G - Bb - D

Eb

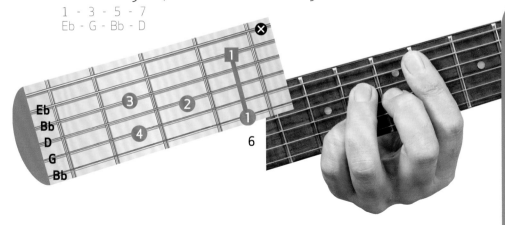

4 # Ebmaj7 (Eb△, Ebmajor7, EbM7)
1 - 3 - 5 - 7
Eb - G - Bb - D

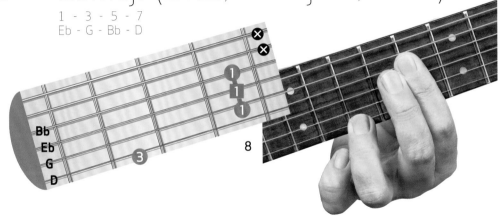

5 # Ebmaj7 (Eb△, Ebmajor7, EbM7)
1 - 3 - 5 - 7
Eb - G - Bb - D

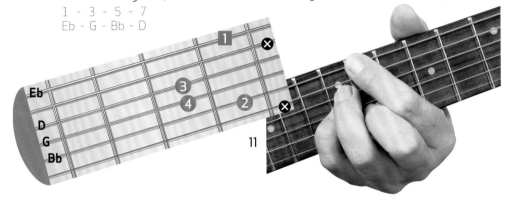

Eb

Eb/D# MAJOR
Ebsus (Eb suspended)

Both variations of the suspended chord (sus2 and sus4) and the related major chord are frequently used in the same chord sequence (e.g. Ebsus4 - Eb - Ebsus2) to create harmonic motion without changing chords. Many great riffs have been based on this idea—The Searchers' "Needles And Pins" and Michael Jackson's "Black Or White" are just two examples.

1 ## Ebsus2
1 - 2 - 5
Eb - F - Bb

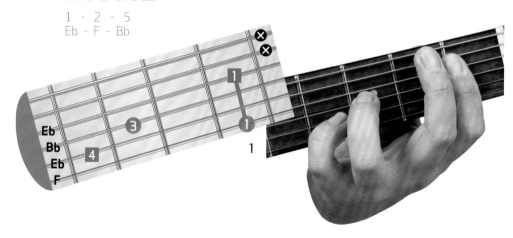

2 ## Ebsus2
1 - 2 - 5
Eb - F - Bb

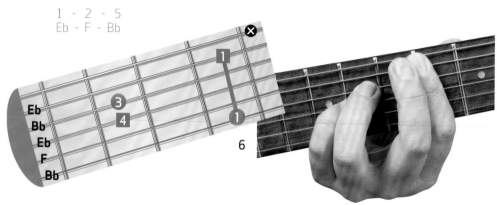

1 Ebsus4
1 - 4 - 5
Eb - Ab - Bb

Eb

2 Ebsus4
1 - 4 - 5
Eb - Ab - Bb

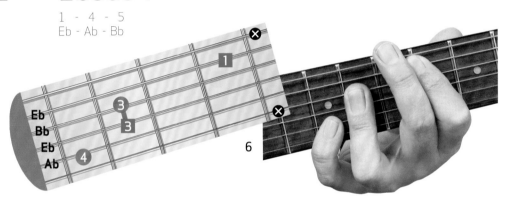

3 Ebsus4
1 - 4 - 5
Eb - Ab - Bb

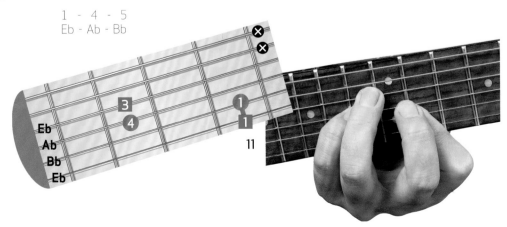

Eb

Eb/D# MINOR

Eb minor is the relative minor of Gb major and shares the same key signature of six flats. Sandwiched between the more "guitar-friendly" keys of D minor and E minor, Eb minor is seldom used in rock and pop music; it is much more predominant in jazz, soul, and funk.
5 A high-register, six-string barre with a big sound and unusual harp-like quality.

---

1 Ebm (Ebmin, Ebminor, Eb−)

1 - b3 - 5
Eb - Gb - Bb

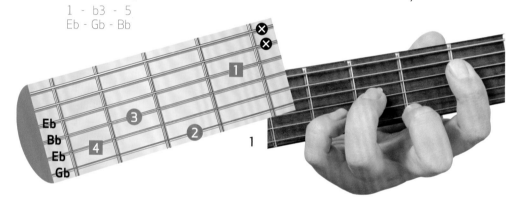

---

2 Ebm (Ebmin, Ebminor, Eb−)

1 - b3 - 5
Eb - Gb - Bb

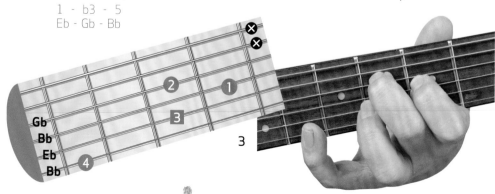

3 Ebm (Ebmin, Ebminor, Eb−)

1 - b3 - 5
Eb - Gb - Bb

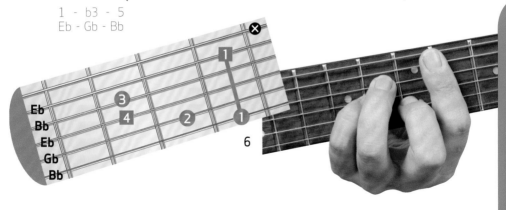

4 Ebm (Ebmin, Ebminor, Eb−)

1 - b3 - 5
Eb - Gb - Bb

5 Ebm (Ebmin, Ebminor, Eb−)

1 - b3 - 5
Eb - Gb - Bb

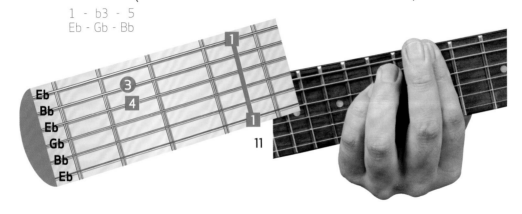

Eb

Eb/D# MINOR

By adding either a sixth or a seventh interval you can change the quality of a minor chord quite significantly. A "straight" Ebm chord has a sad but fairly plain sound; the sixth shifts the chord into more ominous "spy movie theme music" territory, while the minor seventh adds a breezy, light, and jazzy texture.

1 Ebmin6 (Ebminor6, Ebm6, Eb−6)

1 - b3 - 5 - 6
Eb - Gb - Bb - C

2 Ebmin6 (Ebminor6, Ebm6, Eb−6)

1 - b3 - 5 - 6
Eb - Gb - Bb - C

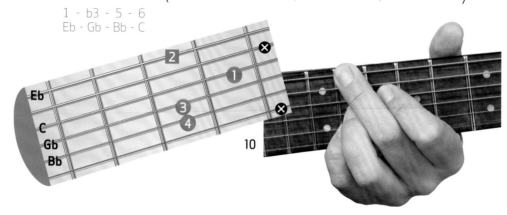

1 Ebmin7 (Ebminor7, Ebm7, Eb−7)

1 - b3 - 5 - b7
Eb - Gb - Bb - Db

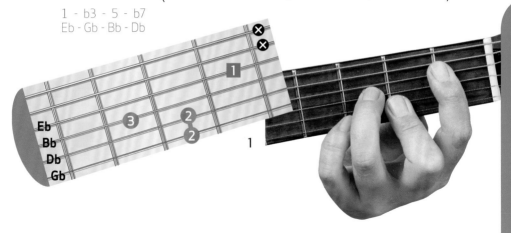

Eb

2 Ebmin7 (Ebminor7, Ebm7, Eb−7)

1 - b3 - 5 - b7
Eb - Gb - Bb - Db

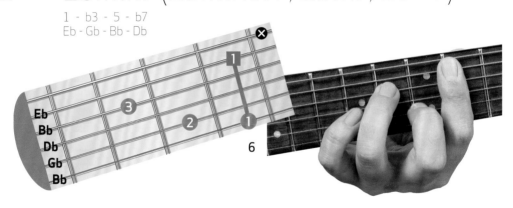

3 Ebmin7 (Ebminor7, Ebm7, Eb−7)

1 - b3 - 5 - b7
Eb - Gb - Bb - Db

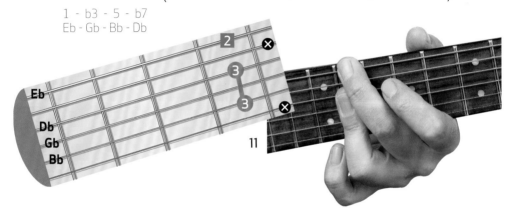

Eb

Eb7/D#7

The dominant seventh in its simplest form is basically a major triad with an added flattened seventh. However, the dominant seventh performs a very different function; it is not a static chord (except in blues progressions), but a motion chord that "pulls" to a major or minor chord with its root a fifth lower. In classical terms, this is the traditional perfect cadence.

1 ## Eb7 (Ebdom7)

1 - 3 - 5 - b7
Eb - G - Bb - Db

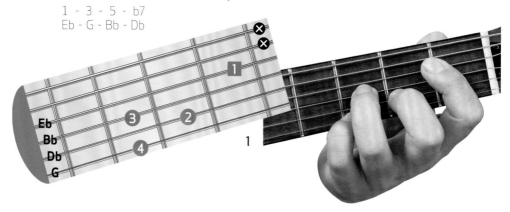

2 ## Eb7 (Ebdom7)

1 - 3 - 5 - b7
Eb - G - Bb - Db

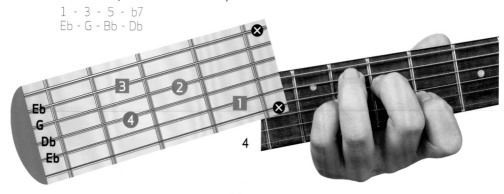

3 Eb7 (Ebdom7)

1 - 3 - 5 - b7
Eb - G - Bb - Db

4 Eb7 (Ebdom7)

1 - 3 - 5 - b7
Eb - G - Bb - Db

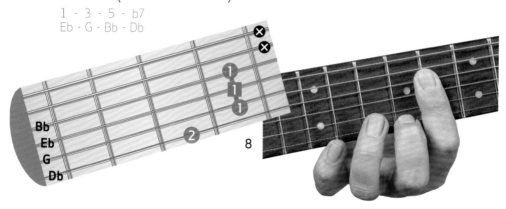

5 Eb7 (Ebdom7)

1 - 3 - 5 - b7
Eb - G - Bb - Db

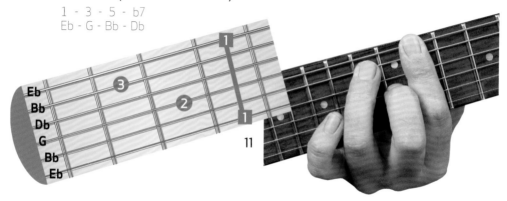

Eb7/D#7

The Eb7#5 chord has a very "dark" sound—perfect for intensifying a V (Eb7#5) to I (Ab) resolution. It can also be used as a chromatic passing chord to create jazzy, contemporary parallel harmonies. Suspended fourths are sometimes added to dominant seventh chords simply to create additional movement within a V–I resolution (e.g. Eb7sus - Eb7 - Ab).

1 Eb7#5 (Eb7aug, Eb7+)

1 - 3 - #5 - b7
Eb - G - B - Db

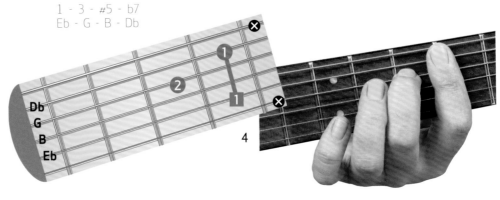

2 Eb7#5 (Eb7aug, Eb7+)

1 - 3 - #5 - b7
Eb - G - B - Db

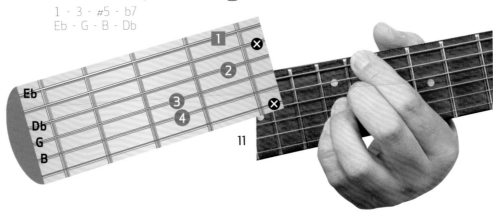

1   Eb7sus (Eb7sus4)

1 - 4 - 5 - b7
Eb - Ab - Bb - Db

2   Eb7sus (Eb7sus4)

1 - 4 - 5 - b7
Eb - Ab - Bb - Db

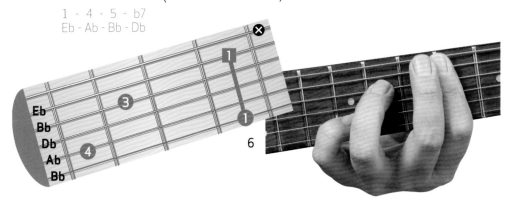

3   Eb7sus (Eb7sus4)

1 - 4 - 5 - b7
Eb - Ab - Bb - Db

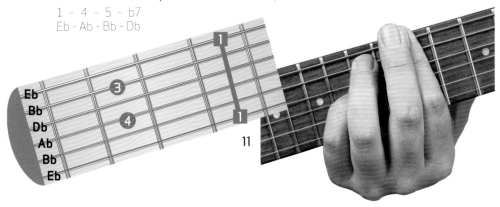

Eb

Eb7/D#7

Dominant seventh chords are often "colored" by adding additional intervals such as ninths and thirteenths.
Eb7b9 A dark sounding, four-string voicing with muted outer strings; resolves perfectly to Ab or Abmajor7.
Eb13: 1 A thirteenth chord inversion with no fifth or ninth and the flattened seventh in the bass.

• ## Eb9 (Ebdom9)

1 - 3 - 5 - b7 - 9
Eb - G - Bb - Db - F

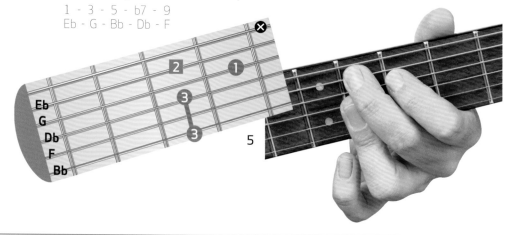

• ## Eb7#9

1 - 3 - 5 - b7 - #9
Eb - G - Bb - Db - F#

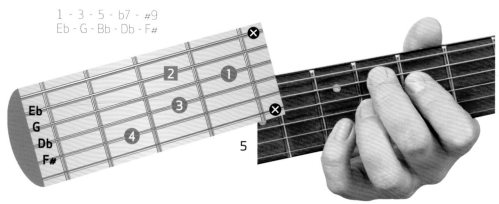

Eb7b9

1 - 3 - 5 - b7 - b9
Eb - G - Bb - Db - Fb

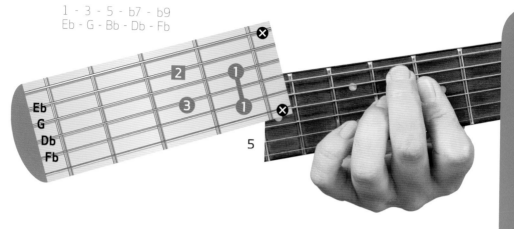

1

Eb13

1 - 3 - 5 - b7 - 9 - 13
Eb - G - Bb - Db - F - C

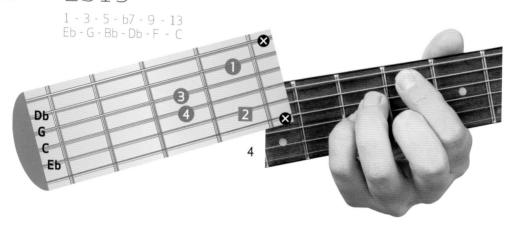

2

Eb13

1 - 3 - 5 - b7 - 9 - 13
Eb - G - Bb - Db - F - C

E

E MAJOR

E major is the original "guitar-friendly" key. The lowest note on the guitar is an E and the lowest root position chord that can be played on the guitar is E major. Many great riffs have revolved around the open first position notes in this key—the bluesy intro of Jimi Hendrix's "Hey Joe" and Johnny Kidd And The Pirates' "Shakin' All Over" are just two examples. **1** One of the most resonant chords on the guitar: the open, six-string E major voicing.

1 E (Emaj, Emajor, EM)

1 - 3 - 5
E - G# - B

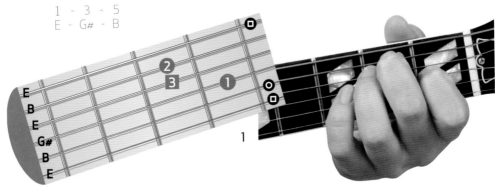

2 E (Emaj, Emajor, EM)

1 - 3 - 5
E - G# - B

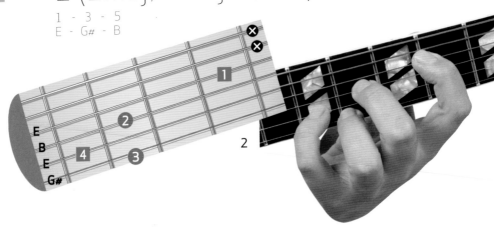

3

E (Emaj, Emajor, EM)

1 - 3 - 5
E - G# - B

4

E (Emaj, Emajor, EM)

1 - 3 - 5
E - G# - B

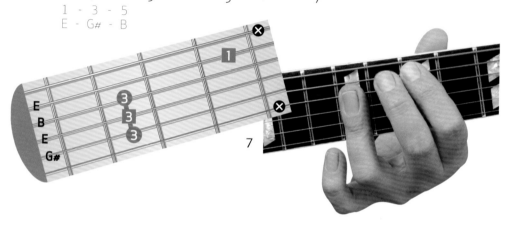

5

E (Emaj, Emajor, EM)

1 - 3 - 5
E - G# - B

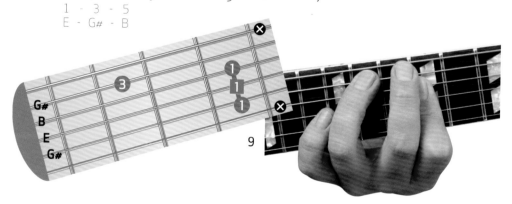

E

E MAJOR

It's an ending chord that's been used by everyone, but the sixth can also be used as a substitute for a basic major chord. **1** A resonant six-string open chord with a tripled root (E) that's perfect for endings. **3** Warm and jazzy, four-string voicing with muted open strings.

1 ## E6 (Emaj6, Emajor6, EM6)

1 - 3 - 5 - 6
E - G# - B - C#

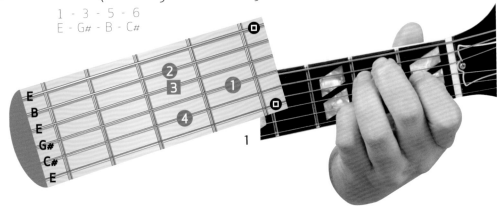

2 ## E6 (Emaj6, Emajor6, EM6)

1 - 3 - 5 - 6
E - G# - B - C#

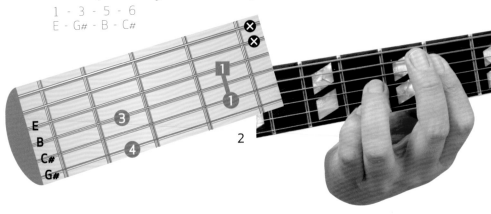

3

E6 (Emaj6, Emajor6, EM6)

1 - 3 - 5 - 6
E - G# - B - C#

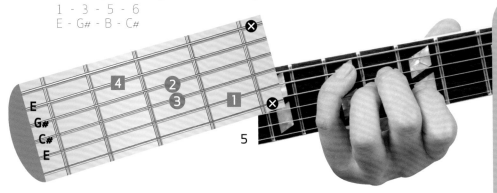

4

E6 (Emaj6, Emajor6, EM6)

1 - 3 - 5 - 6
E - G# - B - C#

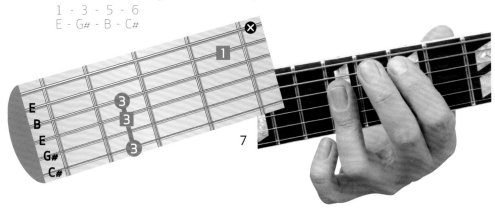

5

E6 (Emaj6, Emajor6, EM6)

1 - 3 - 5 - 6
E - G# - B - C#

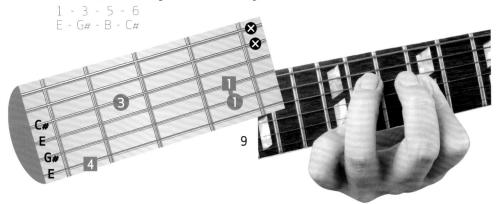

E

E MAJOR

Although essentially a very jazzy chord, the major seventh also features in many rock songs. **1** A huge-sounding, six-string major seventh exclusive to the key of E. **3** Add extra depth to this sweet-sounding, five-string chord by including the low E on the sixth string.

1

Emaj7 (E△, Emajor7, EM7)

1 - 3 - 5 - b7
E - G# - B - D#

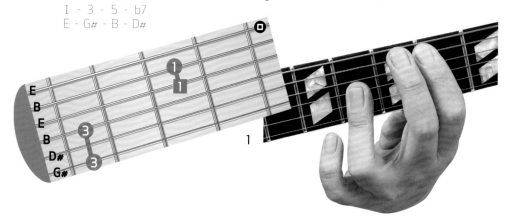

2

Emaj7 (E△, Emajor7, EM7)

1 - 3 - 5 - b7
E - G# - B - D#

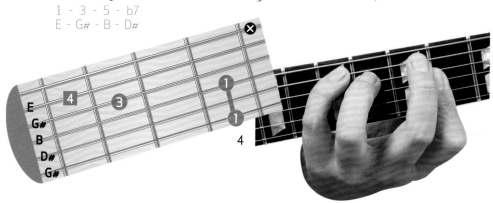

3 Emaj7 (E△, Emajor7, EM7)

1 - 3 - 5 - b7
E - G# - B - D#

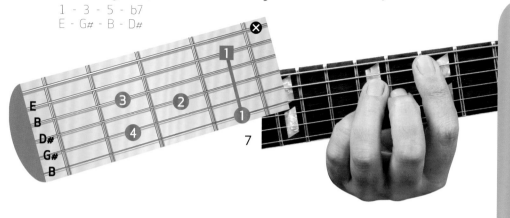

4 Emaj7 (E△, Emajor7, EM7)

1 - 3 - 5 - b7
E - G# - B - D#

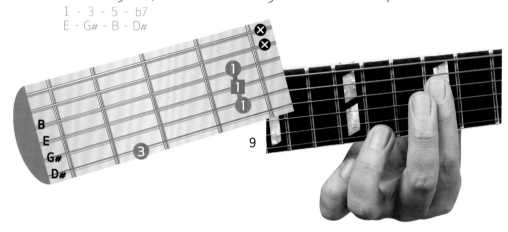

5 Emaj7 (E△, Emajor7, EM7)

1 - 3 - 5 - b7
E - G# - B - D#

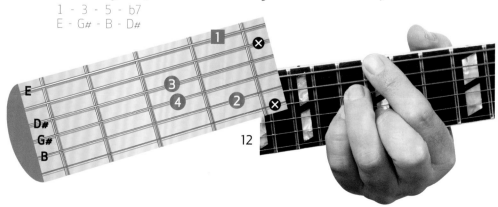

E

E MAJOR
Esus (E suspended)

Suspended chords can be used to add interest to a chord
sequence or static chord vamp, and work well when used in
conjunction with similarly voiced major chords (see pages 86–87).
Esus2: 2 The ubiquitous sus2 barre chord voicing.
Esus4: 1 A full-sounding open chord with a doubled fifth
(B) and trebled root (E).

1 Esus2
1 - 2 - 5
E - F# - B

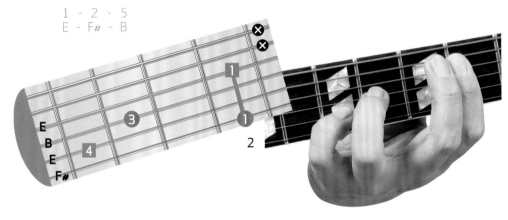

2 Esus2
1 - 2 - 5
E - F# - B

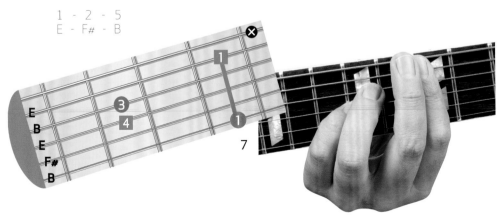

1   # Esus4
1 - 4 - 5
E - A - B

2   # Esus4
1 - 4 - 5
E - A - B

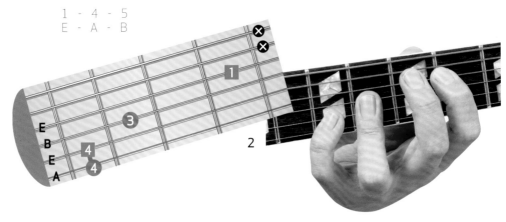

3   # Esus4
1 - 4 - 5
E - A - B

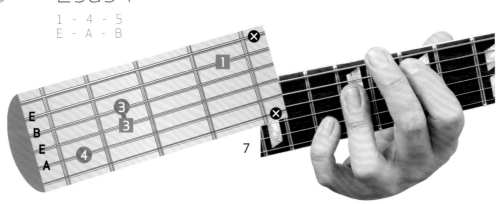

E MINOR

The relative minor of G major, E minor is a common key for minor blues progressions and is frequently used by many guitarists. **1** Full six-string open chord with a big sound generated by a doubled fifth (B) and a tripled root (E). **4** Lighter sounding five-string voicing at the seventh fret; the low E string can be included for more depth.

1 Em (Emin, Eminor, E−)

1 - b3 - 5
E - G - B

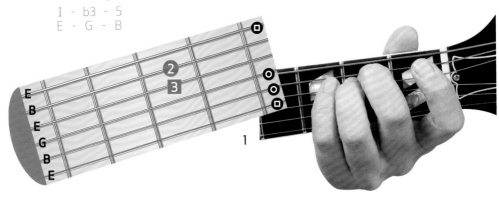

2 Em (Emin, Eminor, E−)

1 - b3 - 5
E - G - B

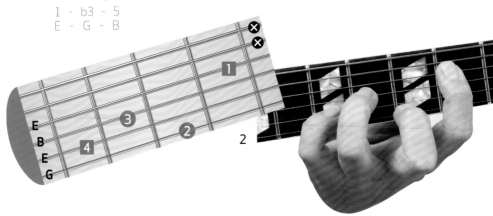

3

Em (Emin, Eminor, E−)

1 - b3 - 5
E - G - B

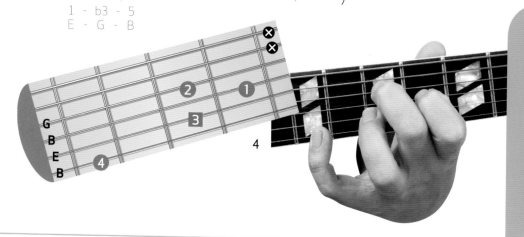

4

Em (Emin, Eminor, E−)

1 - b3 - 5
E - G - B

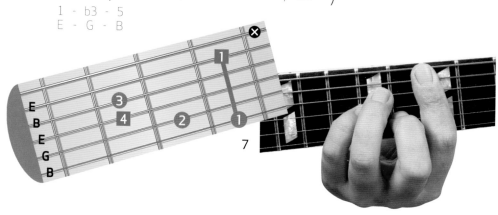

5

Em (Emin, Eminor, E−)

1 - b3 - 5
E - G - B

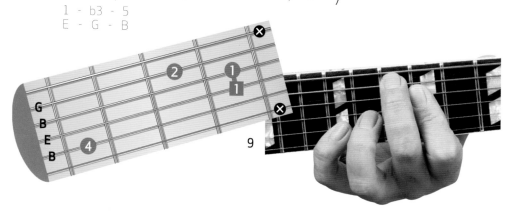

E MINOR

Minor sixth voicings can be used as a substitute for a basic minor chord, while minor seventh chords are great for creating funky chord grooves.
Emin6: 1 A resonant, six-string, open minor sixth with a full sound.
Emin7: 3 High-register, four-string inversion with the fifth (B) as the lowest note.

1 Emin6 (Eminor6, Em6, E−6)

1 - b3 - 5 - 6
E - G - B - C#

2 Emin6 (Eminor6, Em6, E−6)

1 - b3 - 5 - 6
E - G - B - C#

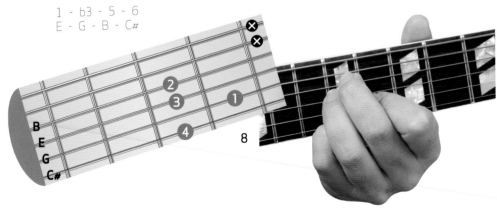

1

Emin7 (Eminor7, Em7, E−7)

1 - b3 - 5 - b7
E - G - B - D

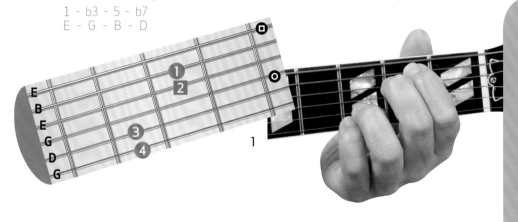

E

2

Emin7 (Eminor7, Em7, E−7)

1 - b3 - 5 - b7
E - G - B - D

3

Emin7 (Eminor7, Em7, E−7)

1 - b3 - 5 - b7
E - G - B - D

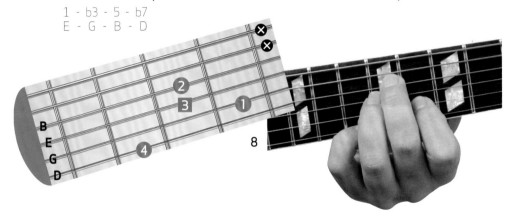

E

E7

These five chords are essential for any blues guitarist. **1** This is the mother of all seventh chords! This open E7 voicing has a doubled seventh (D) for extra bite. **5** This tight-sounding, four-string E7 shape is great for funky rhythm guitar work and can be easily "choked" by simply releasing fretting hand pressure.

1   E7 (Edom7)

1 - 3 - 5 - b7
E - G# - B - D

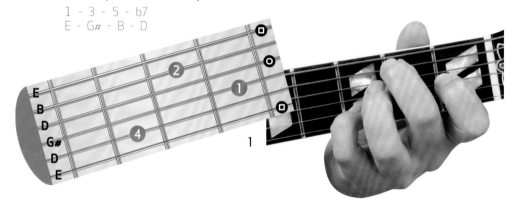

2   E7 (Edom7)

1 - 3 - 5 - b7
E - G# - B - D

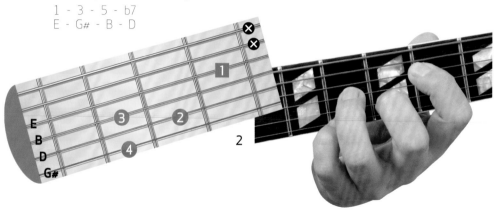

3   E7 (Edom7)

1 - 3 - 5 - b7
E - G# - B - D

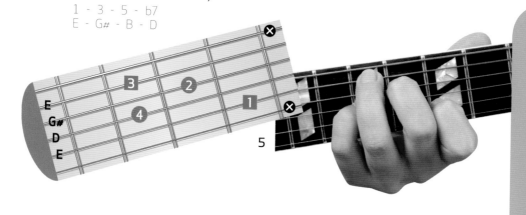

4   E7 (Edom7)

1 - 3 - 5 - b7
E - G# - B - D

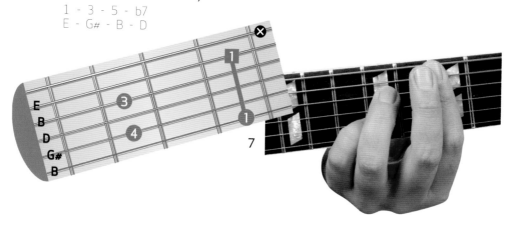

5   E7 (Edom7)

1 - 3 - 5 - b7
E - G# - B - D

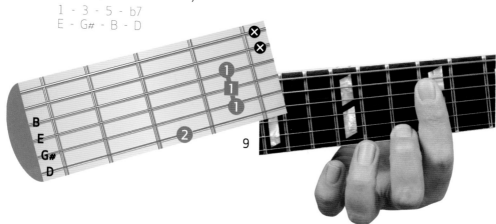

E

E7

Like C7#5 chords, E7#5 chords are "tension creating" dominant seventh chords and are most frequently used in a perfect cadence scenario, i.e. when a dominant chord (V) resolves to its tonic (I).
E7#5: 2 A versatile four-string voicing that was famously used as the opening chord in Chuck Berry's "No Particular Place to Go."
E7sus: 1 A doubled root (E) and fifth (B) result in a big, chiming sound.

1

E7#5 (E7aug, E7+)

1 - 3 - #5 - b7
E - G# - B# - D

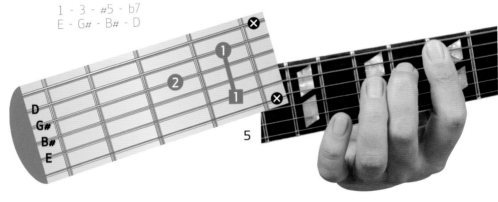

2

E7#5 (E7aug, E7+)

1 - 3 - #5 - b7
E - G# - B# - D

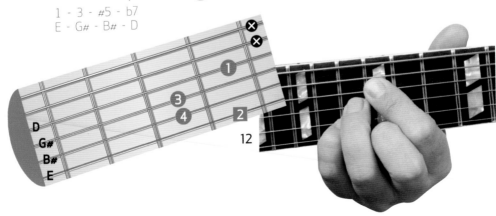

1   E7sus (E7sus4)

1 - 4 - 5 - b7
E - A - B - D

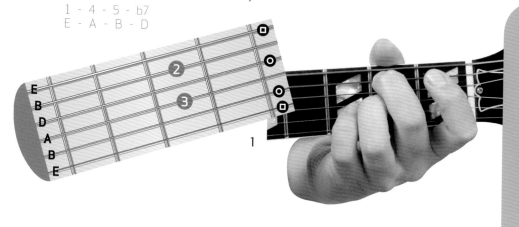

2   E7sus (E7sus4)

1 - 4 - 5 - b7
E - A - B - D

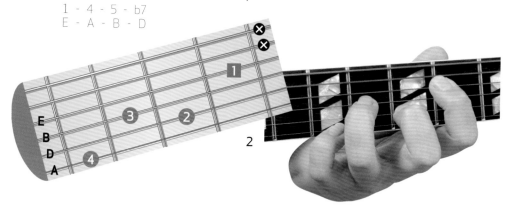

3   E7sus (E7sus4)

1 - 4 - 5 - b7
E - A - B - D

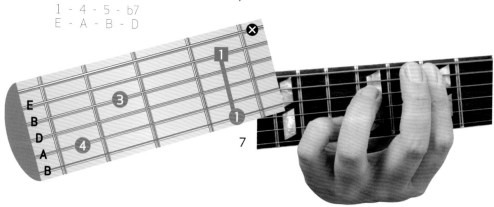

E

E7

A selection of dominant sevenths with various "color tensions" added to create harmonic interest.

E7#9 This shape, often referred to as the "Hendrix chord," is actually the first chord of the "Purple Haze" verse sequence.

E13: 2 A funky five-note thirteenth chord that also includes the ninth for extra harmonic color.

E9 (Edom9)

1 - 3 - 5 - b7 - 9
E - G# - B - D - F#

E7#9

1 - 3 - 5 - b7 - #9
E - G# - B - D - F##

E7b9

1 - 3 - 5 - b7 - b9
E - G# - B - D - F

E

1   E13

1 - 3 - 5 - b7 - 9 - 13
E - G# - B - D - F# - C#

2   E13

1 - 3 - 5 - b7 - 9 - 13
E - G# - B - D - F# - C#

F

F MAJOR

Due to a lack of open chord shapes, F major is not a particularly "guitar-friendly" key; it is, however, frequently used since it is a popular key with vocalists and horn players. **1** The lowest full six-string barre shape on the neck has a big sound, but requires a strong fretting hand. **4** Another useful barre, this time a four-string variant, and frequently used by rock guitarists.

1 F (Fmaj, Fmajor, FM)

1 - 3 - 5
F - A - C

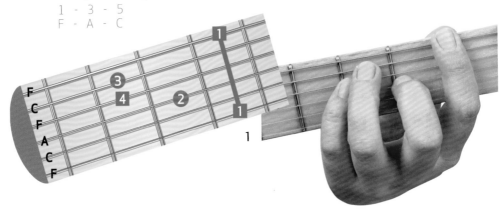

2 F (Fmaj, Fmajor, FM)

1 - 3 - 5
F - A - C

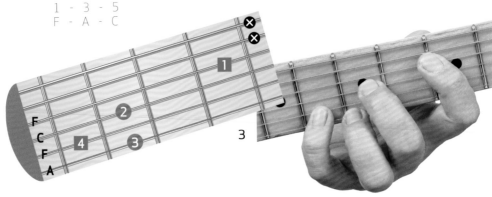

3 F (Fmaj, Fmajor, FM)

1 - 3 - 5
F - A - C

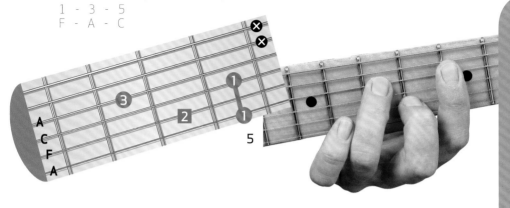

4 F (Fmaj, Fmajor, FM)

1 - 3 - 5
F - A - C

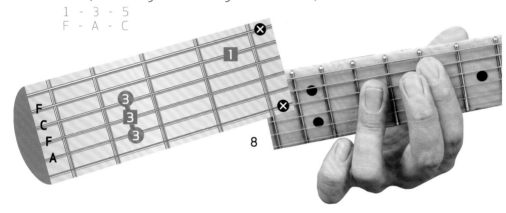

5 F (Fmaj, Fmajor, FM)

1 - 3 - 5
F - A - C

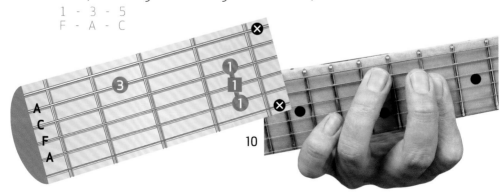

F

F MAJOR

Sixth chords add the interval of a sixth to the basic major triad, hence the 1 - 3 - 5 - 6 harmonic spelling of these chords. **1** Four-string, root position voicing ideal for funky blues rhythm guitar. **3** Mellow and jazzy, four-string chord with muted outer strings.

1 F6 (Fmaj6, Fmajor6, FM6)

1 - 3 - 5 - 6
F - A - C - D

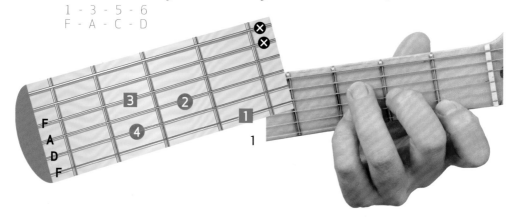

2 F6 (Fmaj6, Fmajor6, FM6)

1 - 3 - 5 - 6
F - A - C - D

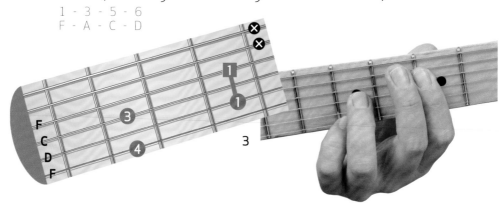

3 F6 (Fmaj6, Fmajor6, FM6)

1 - 3 - 5 - 6
F - A - C - D

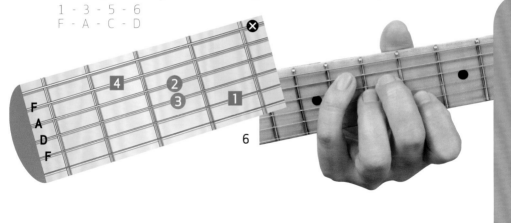

4 F6 (Fmaj6, Fmajor6, FM6)

1 - 3 - 5 - 6
F - A - C - D

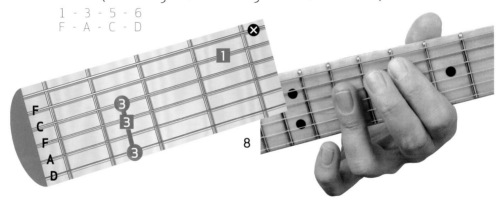

5 F6 (Fmaj6, Fmajor6, FM6)

1 - 3 - 5 - 6
F - A - C - D

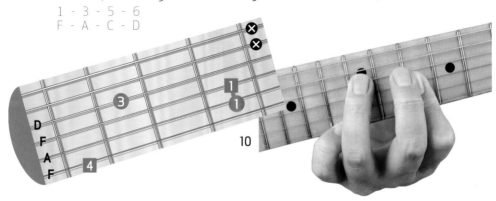

F MAJOR

The smooth-sounding major seventh chord adds color to any progression. **1** This four-note, high-register open major seventh sounds great when picked and is famously used in the intro of Led Zeppelin's epic "Stairway To Heaven." **3** A piano-style, "closed" five-string voicing with doubled third.

1 Fmaj7 (FΔ, Fmajor7, FM7)

1 - 3 - 5 - 7
F - A - C - E

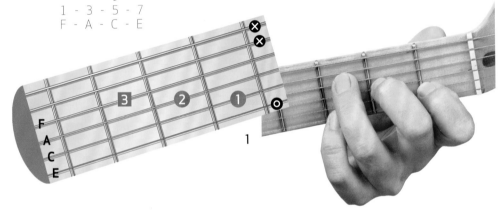

2 Fmaj7 (FΔ, Fmajor7, FM7)

1 - 3 - 5 - 7
F - A - C - E

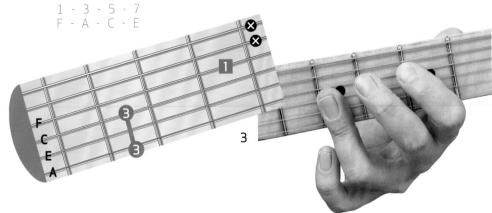

3   # Fmaj7 (F△, Fmajor7, FM7)
1 - 3 - 5 - 7
F - A - C - E

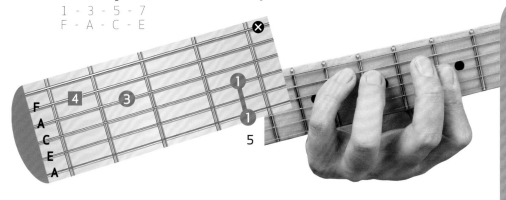

4   # Fmaj7 (F△, Fmajor7, FM7)
1 - 3 - 5 - 7
F - A - C - E

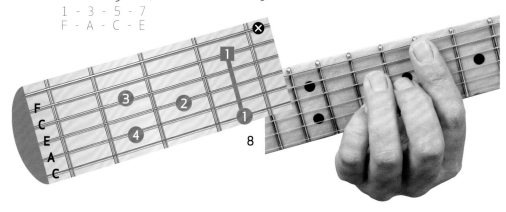

5   # Fmaj7 (F△, Fmajor7, FM7)
1 - 3 - 5 - 7
F - A - C - E

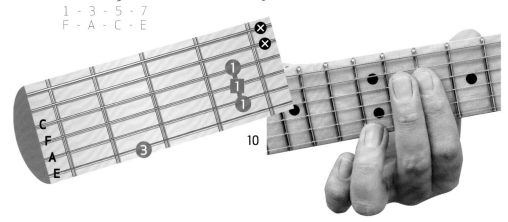

F MAJOR
Fsus (F suspended)

Suspended chords can be used to create harmonic ambiguity;
with no third, they are neither major nor minor.
Fsus2: 1 A first-position, five-string voicing that makes use of the
open third string.
Fsus4: 1 You can create a big sound with this six-string sus4 voicing
—it works well when resolved to F major, shape 1 on page 104.

1 ## Fsus2

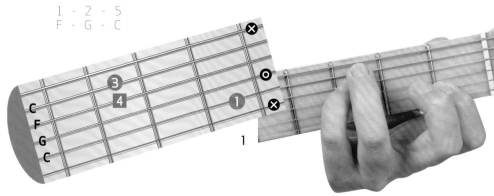

2 ## Fsus2

1 - 2 - 5
F - G - C

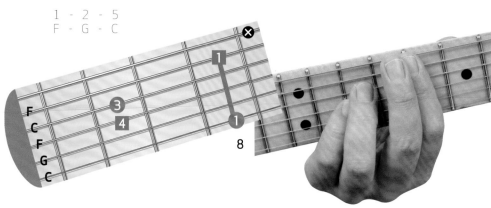

1 ## Fsus4

1 - 4 - 5
F - Bb - C

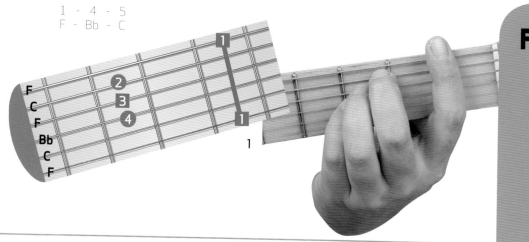

2 ## Fsus4

1 - 4 - 5
F - Bb - C

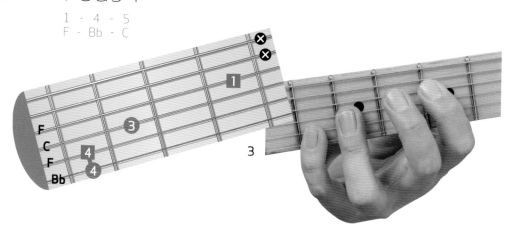

3 ## Fsus4

1 - 4 - 5
F - Bb - C

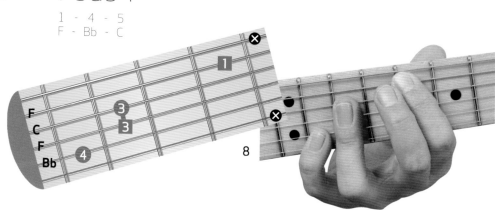

F

F MINOR

The key of F minor (which contains four flats) is the relative key of Ab major and is more prevalent in jazz and related genres since it is a good key for horn players. **1** A big full sound can be achieved with this low six-string barre, but it needs plenty of fretting hand strength. **5** A four-string inversion played on the inner strings with the minor third as the lowest note.

1 ## Fm (Fmin, Fminor, F−)

1 - b3 - 5
F - Ab - C

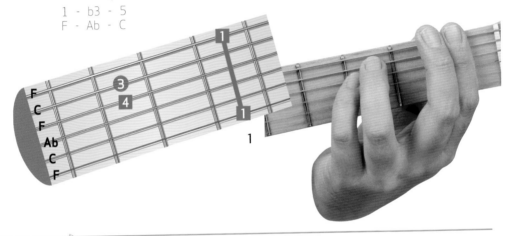

2 ## Fm (Fmin, Fminor, F−)

1 - b3 - 5
F - Ab - C

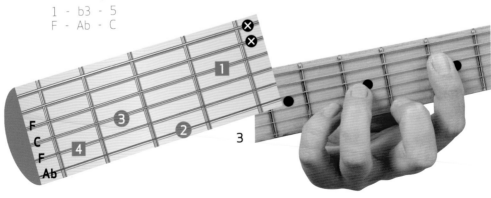

3

Fm (Fmin, Fminor, F−)

1 - b3 - 5
F - Ab - C

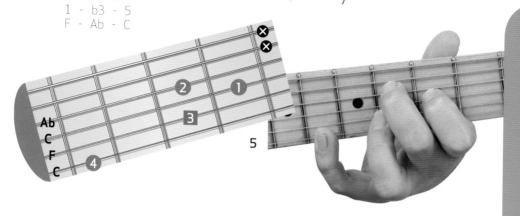

4

Fm (Fmin, Fminor, F−)

1 - b3 - 5
F - Ab - C

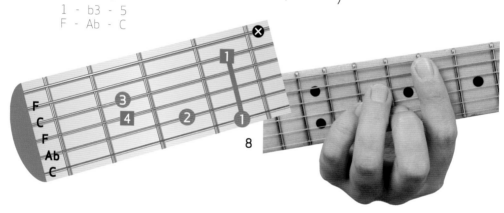

5

Fm (Fmin, Fminor, F−)

1 - b3 - 5
F - Ab - C

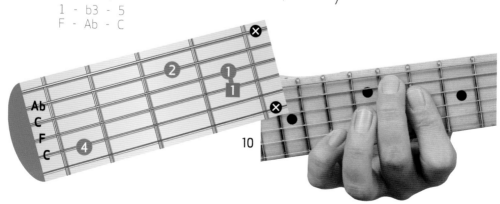

F

F MINOR

Adding the sixth or the flattened seventh to a basic minor triad is a great way to introduce some color to an otherwise plain-sounding chord.
Fmin6: 1 This four-string inversion with the fifth (C) in the bass has a spooky, ominous quality.
Fmin7: 3 An incredibly versatile minor 7th voicing with a doubled 5th (C).

1

Fmin6 (Fminor6, Fm6, F−6)

1 - b3 - 5 - 6
F - Ab - C - D

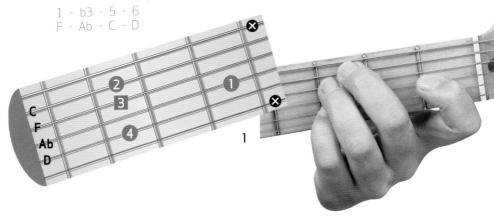

2

Fmin6 (Fminor6, Fm6, F−6)

1 - b3 - 5 - 6
F - Ab - C - D

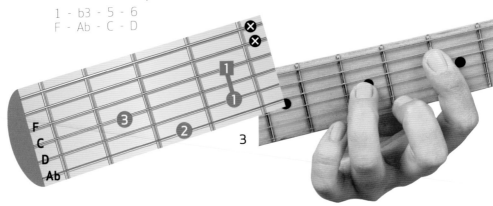

1

Fmin7 (Fminor7, Fm7, F−7)

1 - b3 - 5 - b7
F - Ab - C - Eb

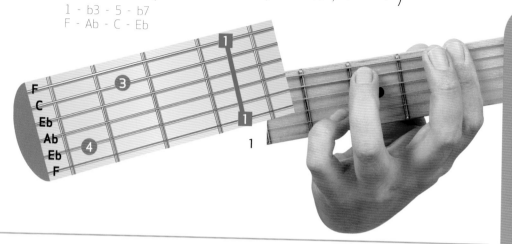

2

Fmin7 (Fminor7, Fm7, F−7)

1 - b3 - 5 - b7
F - Ab - C - Eb

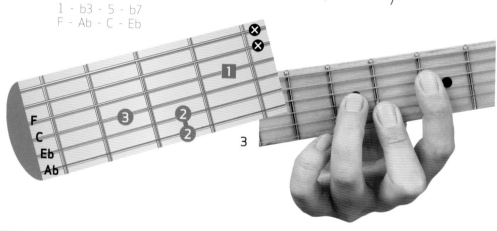

3

Fmin7 (Fminor7, Fm7, F−7)

1 - b3 - 5 - b7
F - Ab - C - Eb

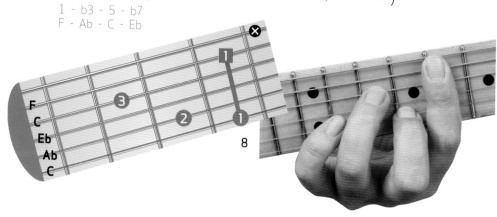

F7

A dominant seventh can be used as a static chord (e.g. the first chord of a blues), or as a "going home" cadence chord. F7 can resolve to either Bb major or Bb minor. **1** The lowest F7 shape on the neck has a big sound but requires a strong fretting hand. **3** This four-note seventh voicing is a favorite among fingerstyle guitarists who often add the low fifth (C) on the sixth string to create an alternating bassline.

1 ## F7 (Fdom7)

1 - 3 - 5 - b7
F - A - C - Eb

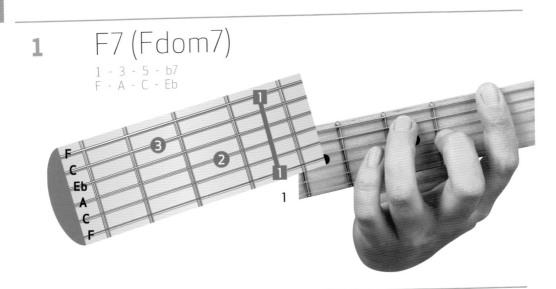

2 ## F7 (Fdom7)

1 - 3 - 5 - b7
F - A - C - Eb

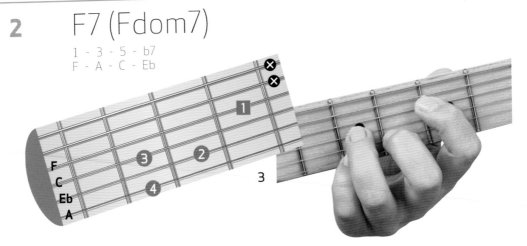

3 F7 (Fdom7)

1 - 3 - 5 - b7
F - A - C - Eb

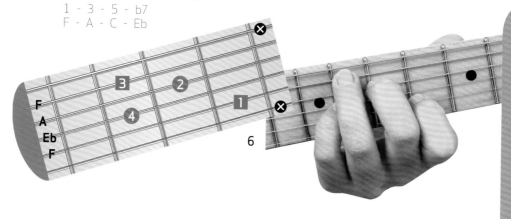

4 F7 (Fdom7)

1 - 3 - 5 - b7
F - A - C - Eb

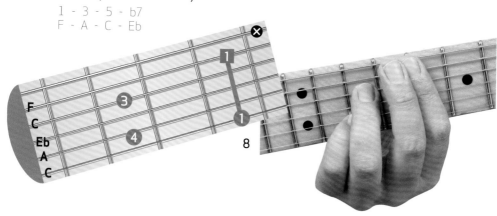

5 F7 (Fdom7)

1 - 3 - 5 - b7
F - A - C - Eb

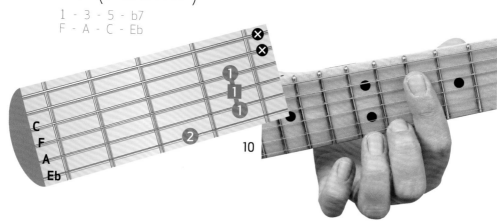

F

F7

Adding a sharpened fifth to a dominant seventh chord creates tension and heightens the "pull" back to the home chord in a perfect (V–I) cadence. **F7#5: 2** A dark and moody inversion with the flattened seventh (Eb) in the bass. **F7sus: 2** This high-register, four-string root position chord is ideal for syncopated rhythm work (try "choking" the chord by releasing the pressure of your fretting hand for a staccato sound).

1   F7#5 (F7aug, F7+)

1 - 3 - #5 - b7
F - A - C# - Eb

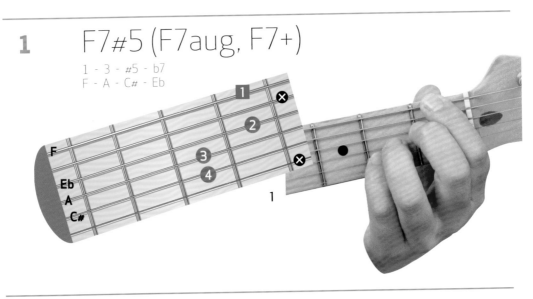

2   F7#5 (F7aug, F7+)

1 - 3 - #5 - b7
F - A - C# - Eb

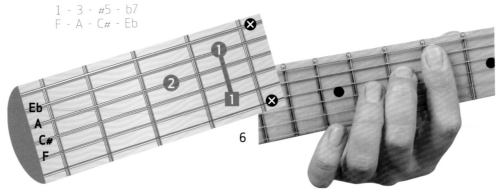

1 F7sus (F7sus4)

1 - 4 - 5 - b7
F - Bb - C - Eb

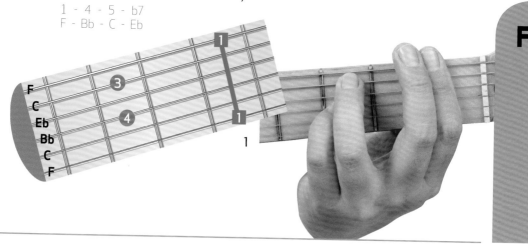

2 F7sus (F7sus4)

1 - 4 - 5 - b7
F - Bb - C - Eb

3 F7sus (F7sus4)

1 - 4 - 5 - b7
F - Bb - C - Eb

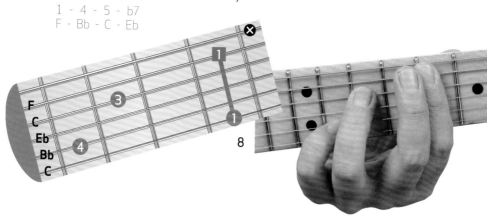

F7

Ninths can create additional harmonic interest when added to a dominant seventh. Altered ninth voicings (#9/b9) create tension and heighten the resolution when used in a perfect (V–1) cadence; natural ninth chords are frequently used as a static vamp chord in blues and funk tunes. The jazzy thirteenth is a very versatile chord and is used in many genres.

F9 (Fdom9)

1 - 3 - 5 - b7 - 9
F - A - C - Eb - G

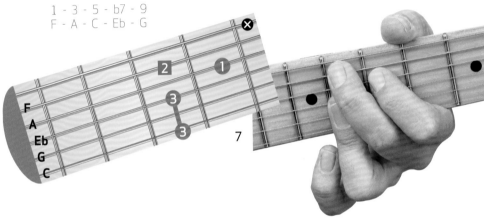

F7#9

1 - 3 - 5 - b7 - #9
F - A - C - Eb - G#

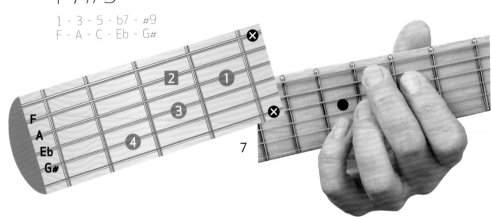

F7b9

1 - 3 - 5 - b7 - b9
F - A - C - Eb - Gb

F

1   F13

1 - 3 - 5 - b7 - 9 - 13
F - A - C - Eb - G - D

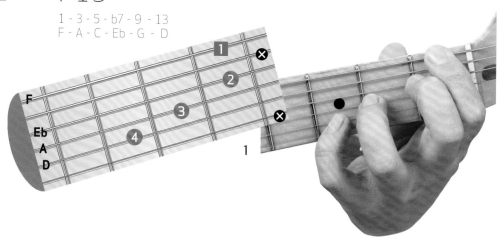

2   F13

1 - 3 - 5 - b7 - 9 - 13
F - A - C - Eb - G - D

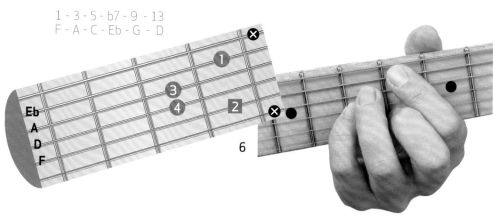

F#/Gb MAJOR

Not an obvious guitar key with its lack of open chords (and six sharps in the key signature), F# is nonetheless a popular key in the rock genre due to the low open E, which can be incorporated into chord-based riffs. **1** Full six-string barre with a big sound, which is ideal for strummed rhythms. **3** Four-string inversion with its third (A#) in the bass—great for "choked" rhythm work since it can be easily damped.

1 F# (F#maj, F#major, F#M)

1 - 3 - 5
F# - A# - C#

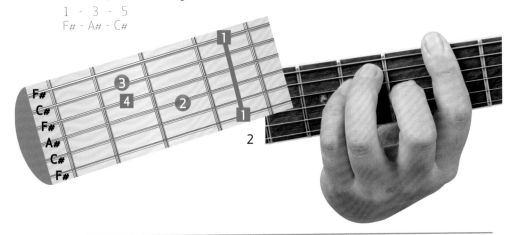

2 F# (F#maj, F#major, F#M)

1 - 3 - 5
F# - A# - C#

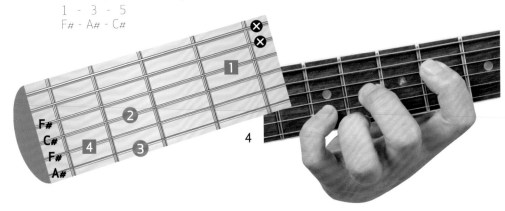

3 F# (F#maj, F#major, F#M)
1 - 3 - 5
F# - A# - C#

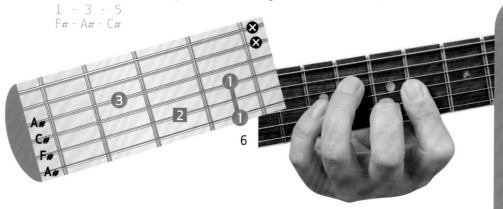

4 F# (F#maj, F#major, F#M)
1 - 3 - 5
F# - A# - C#

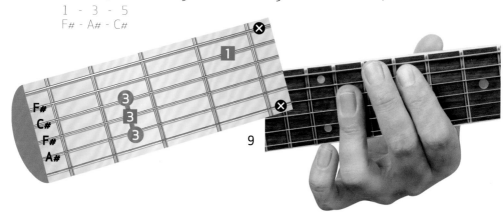

5 F# (F#maj, F#major, F#M)
1 - 3 - 5
F# - A# - C#

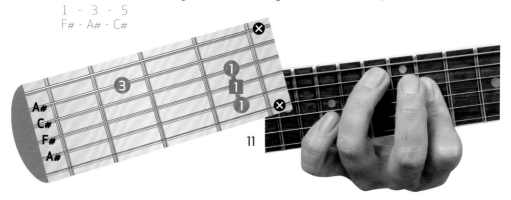

F#/Gb MAJOR

This chord is a good substitute for a basic major chord, since the sixth interval will not clash with a tonic melody note (unlike the seventh in a major seventh chord). **1** A bright but warm high-register voicing that is great for "choked" soul and funk comps. **4** A full-sounding, five-string voicing that makes an ideal ending chord.

1

F#6 (F#maj6, F#major6, F#M6)

1 - 3 - 5 - 6
F# - A# - C# - D#

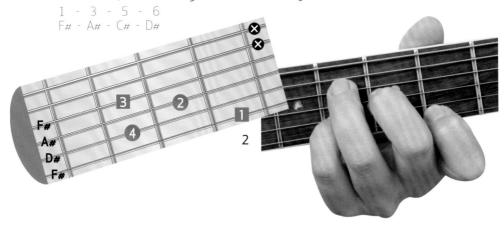

2

F#6 (F#maj6, F#major6, F#M6)

1 - 3 - 5 - 6
F# - A# - C# - D#

3 F#6 (F#maj6, F#major6, F#M6)

1 - 3 - 5 - 6
F# - A# - C# - D#

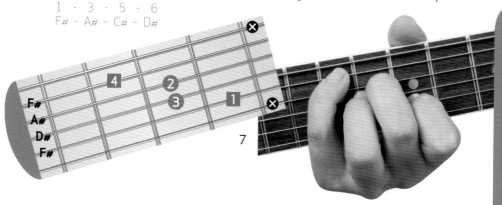

4 F#6 (F#maj6, F#major6, F#M6)

1 - 3 - 5 - 6
F# - A# - C# - D#

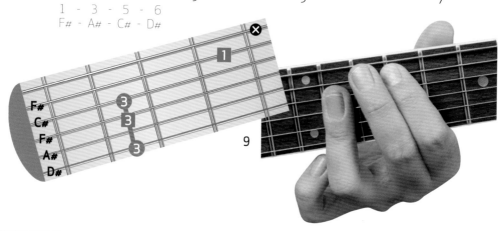

5 F#6 (F#maj6, F#major6, F#M6)

1 - 3 - 5 - 6
F# - A# - C# - D#

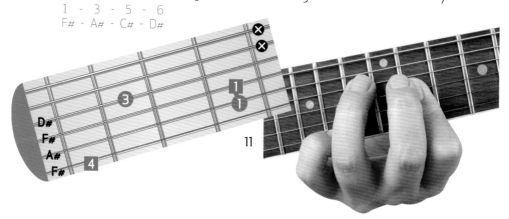

F#/Gb MAJOR

Although the major seventh chord is often ignored by rock guitarists because of its jazzy connotations, this bright, breezy sounding chord actually works well in rock. **1** Subtle "closed" piano-style, four-string voicing. **5** A bright, high-register inversion with the fifth (C#) in the bass.

1 F#maj7 (F#△, F#major7, F#M7)

1 - 3 - 5 - 7
F# - A# - C# - E#

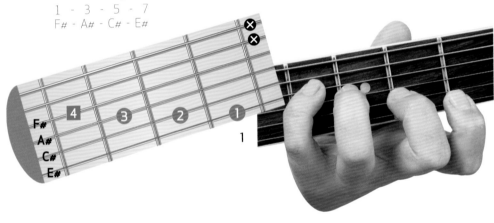

2 F#maj7 (F#△, F#major7, F#M7)

1 - 3 - 5 - 7
F# - A# - C# - E#

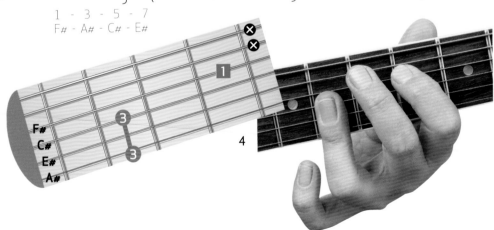

3

F#maj7 (F#△, F#major7, F#M7)

1 - 3 - 5 - 7
F# - A# - C# - E#

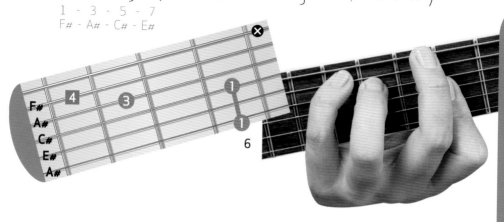

4

F#maj7 (F#△, F#major7, F#M7)

1 - 3 - 5 - 7
F# - A# - C# - E#

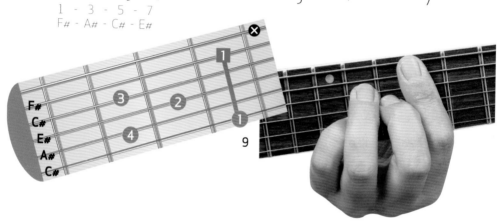

5

F#maj7 (F#△, F#major7, F#M7)

1 - 3 - 5 - 7
F# - A# - C# - E#

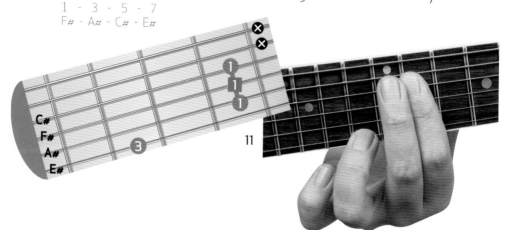

F#/Gb MAJOR
F#sus (F# suspended)

A suspended chord temporarily "suspends" the third of a chord by replacing it with the second or the fourth—this is then resolved by reverting to the major chord, or simply left "hanging" to intensify harmonic tension.
F#sus2: 1 Bright and percussive four-string shape ideal for crisp rhythm work.
F#sus4: 2 Ideal for static chord vamps when partnered with F# major, shape 2 on page 122.

1 ## F#sus2

1 - 2 - 5
F# - G# - C#

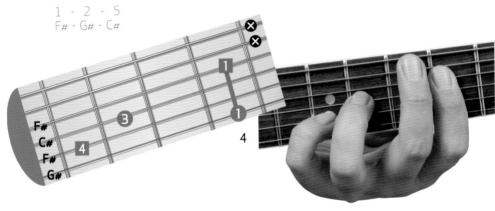

2 ## F#sus2

1 - 2 - 5
F# - G# - C#

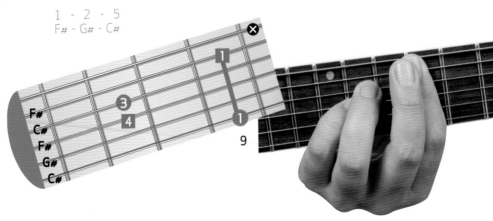

1 F#sus4

1 - 4 - 5
F# - B - C#

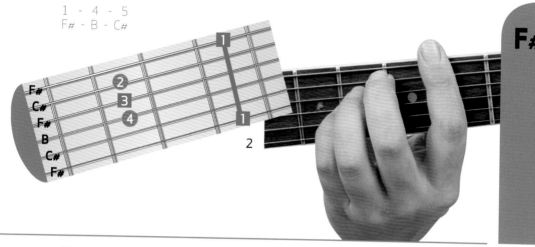

2 F#sus4

1 - 4 - 5
F# - B - C#

3 F#sus4

1 - 4 - 5
F# - B - C#

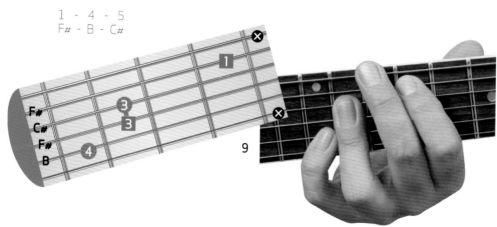

F#

F#/Gb MINOR

Since it is the relative minor of A major, F# minor chords occur in many songs. There are no open chord shapes for this key, so these five shapes are essential weapons to include in your chord armory! **1** A big, full sound can be achieved with this low six-string barre, but it needs plenty of fretting hand strength. **4** A less tricky shape, this five-string barre is quite easy to play and great for percussive rhythm work.

1 ## F#m (F#min, F#minor, F#-)

1 - b3 - 5
F# - A - C#

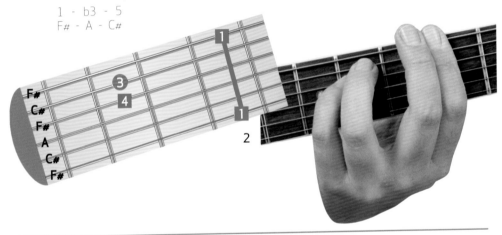

2 ## F#m (F#min, F#minor, F#-)

1 - b3 - 5
F# - A - C#

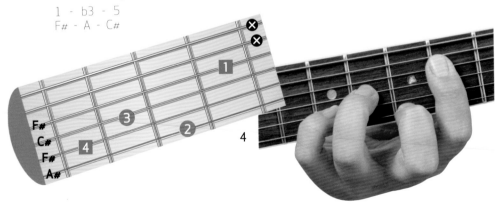

3 F#m (F#min, F#minor, F#-)

1 - b3 - 5
F# - A - C#

4 F#m (F#min, F#minor, F#-)

1 - b3 - 5
F# - A - C#

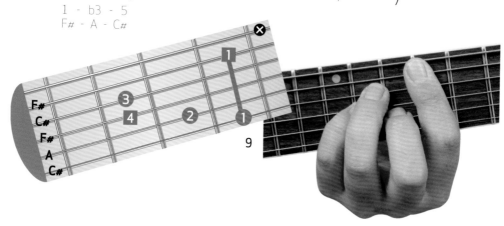

5 F#m (F#min, F#minor, F#-)

1 - b3 - 5
F# - A - C#

F#

F#/Gb MINOR

Experimenting with chord voicings by adding a sixth or a seventh
to a basic minor chord will help you to create more exciting accompaniments.
F#min6: 1 A dark and evocative four-string shape with muted outer strings.
F#min7: 2 A light and breezy, high-register, four-string chord voicing.

1 ## F#min6 (F#minor6, F#m6, F#-6)

1 - b3 - 5 - 6
F# - A - C# - D#

2 ## F#min6 (F#minor6, F#m6, F#-6)

1 - b3 - 5 - 6
F# - A - C# - D#

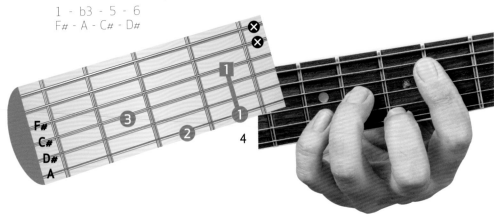

1 F#min7 (F#minor7, F#m7, F#-7)

1 - b3 - 5 - b7
F# - A - C# - E

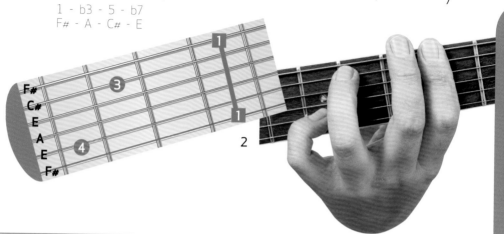

2 F#min7 (F#minor7, F#m7, F#-7)

1 - b3 - 5 - b7
F# - A - C# - E

3 F#min7 (F#minor7, F#m7, F#-7)

1 - b3 - 5 - b7
F# - A - C# - E

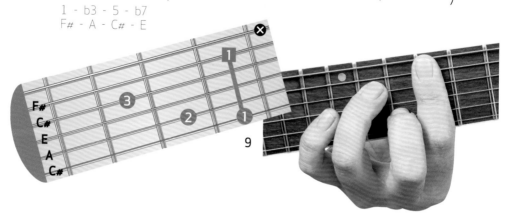

F#

F#7/Gb7

The dominant seventh chord is the most powerful chord in Western music; built on the fifth step of the major or harmonic minor scale, it resolves onto its tonic chord (e.g. F#7 resolves to B or B minor). Composers skilfully manipulate this resolution tendency to create harmonic movement. **3** The classic four-note seventh chord with doubled root and omitted fifth based on an open C7 shape.

1 F#7 (F#dom7)

1 - 3 - 5 - b7
F# - A# - C# - E

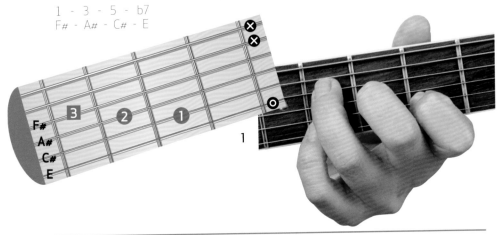

2 F#7 (F#dom7)

1 - 3 - 5 - b7
F# - A# - C# - E

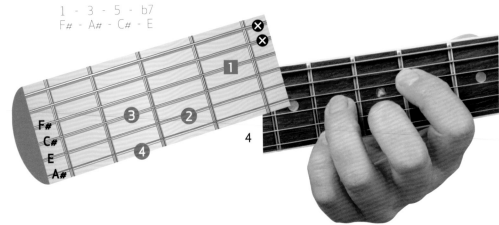

3   ## F#7 (F#dom7)
1 - 3 - 5 - b7
F# - A# - C# - E

7

4   ## F#7 (F#dom7)
1 - 3 - 5 - b7
F# - A# - C# - E

9

5   ## F#7 (F#dom7)
1 - 3 - 5 - b7
F# - A# - C# - E

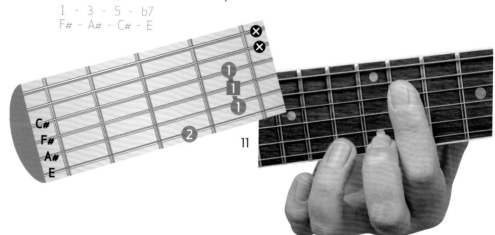

11

F#

F#7/Gb7

Sharpening the fifth of a dominant seventh results in a much darker sounding chord, which is often used to create extra tension when the chord is used in a V (C#7) to I (F#) scenario. Suspending the fourth creates a less intense sense of anticipation.

F#7#5: 1 A jazzy four-string voicing with muted first and fifth strings.

F#7sus: 3 A tight and funky chord—great for rhythm work when paired with F#7, shape 4 on page 135.

1 F#7#5 (F#7aug, F#7+)

1 - 3 - #5 - b7
F# - A# - C## - E

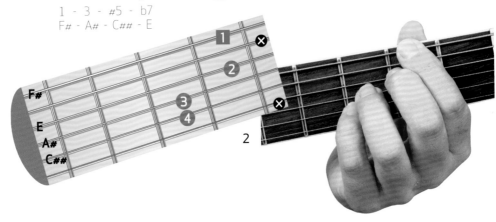

2 F#7#5 (F#7aug, F#7+)

1 - 3 - #5 - b7
F# - A# - C## - E

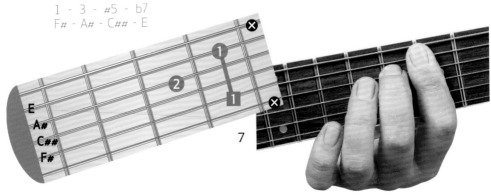

1   F#7sus (F#7sus4)
1 - 4 - 5 - b7
F# - B - C# - E

2   F#7sus (F#7sus4)
1 - 4 - 5 - b7
F# - B - C# - E

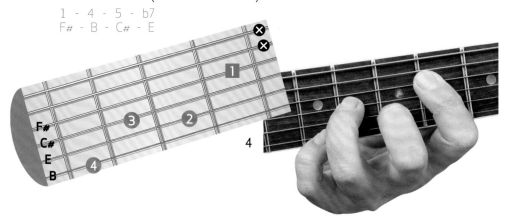

3   F#7sus (F#7sus4)
1 - 4 - 5 - b7
F# - B - C# - E

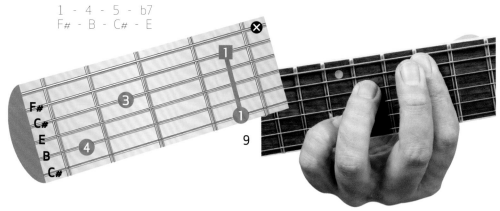

F#7/Gb7

Ninth chords add extra color to the dominant seventh by adding a ninth to the chord. The thirteenth chord stacks another interval onto the ninth chord which results in a six-note chord.
F#9 Five-string, high-register voicing perfect for funk guitar styles.
F#13: 1 Deep and jazzy, four-string chord with muted first and fifth strings.

F#9 (F#dom9)

1 - 3 - 5 - b7 - 9
F# - A# - C# - E - G#

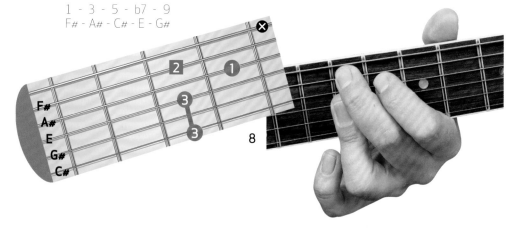

F#7#9

1 - 3 - 5 - b7 - #9
F# - A# - C# - E - G##

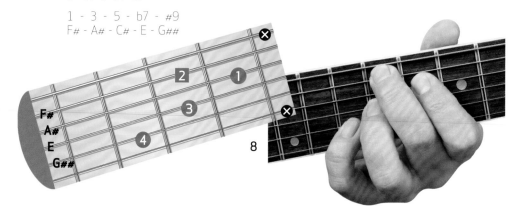

F#7b9

1 - 3 - 5 - b7 - b9
F# - A# - C# - E - G

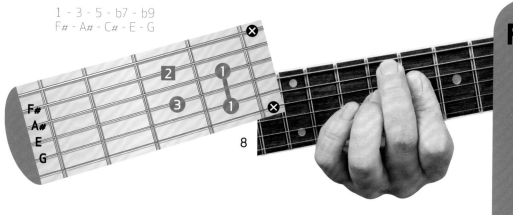

1

F#13

1 - 3 - 5 - b7 - 9 - 13
F# - A# - C# - E - G# - D#

2

F#13

1 - 3 - 5 - b7 - 9 - 13
F# - A# - C# - E - G# - D#

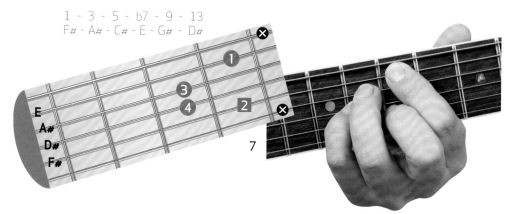

G

G MAJOR

Each key has its own distinct musical characteristic and flavor; Albert Lavignac describes G major as a "rural, merry" key in his famous book, *Music and Musicians*, written in 1905. Perhaps this explains why it is such a popular key for folk and country music. The three primary chords (G, C, and D) of G major are also all available as open shapes—making this an appealing key for beginners, songwriters, and fingerpickers alike.

1   G (Gmaj, Gmajor, GM)

1 - 3 - 5
G - B - D

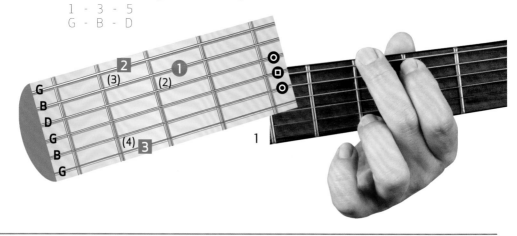

2   G (Gmaj, Gmajor, GM)

1 - 3 - 5
G - B - D

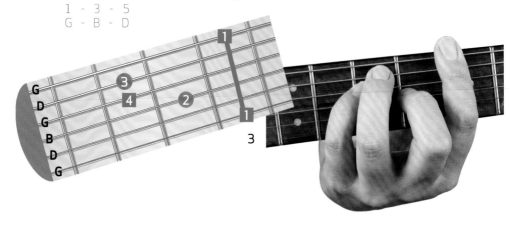

3 G (Gmaj, Gmajor, GM)

1 - 3 - 5
G - B - D

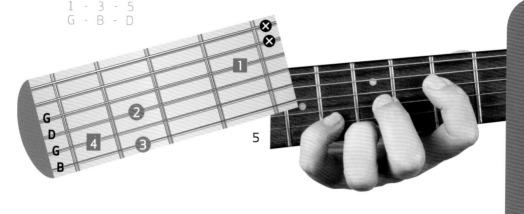

4 G (Gmaj, Gmajor, GM)

1 - 3 - 5
G - B - D

5 G (Gmaj, Gmajor, GM)

1 - 3 - 5
G - B - D

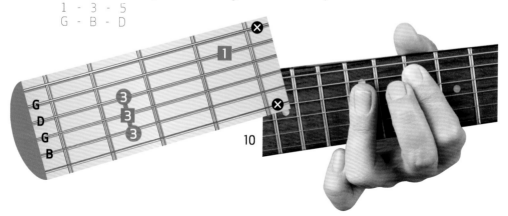

G MAJOR

The sixth interval is often added to a major chord to create extra harmonic interest; the sixth is a benign interval that can be safely added to a major chord since it harmonizes a sustained tonic melody note; this makes it a great chord for a final cadence (ending). **1** This six-note, resonant chord contains four open strings—perfect for that "big" ending.

1 G6 (Gmaj6, Gmajor6, GM6)

1 - 3 - 5 - 6
G - B - D - E

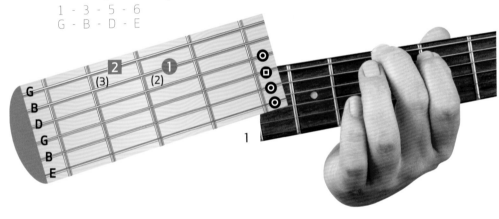

2 G6 (Gmaj6, Gmajor6, GM6)

1 - 3 - 5 - 6
G - B - D - E

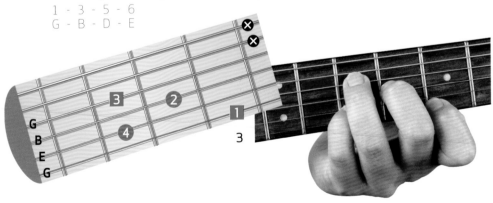

3   G6 (Gmaj6, Gmajor6, GM6)

1 - 3 - 5 - 6
G - B - D - E

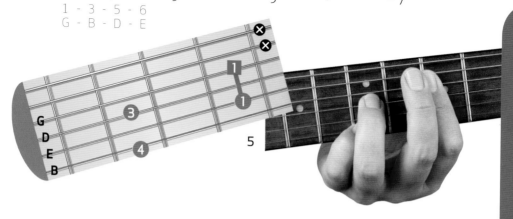

4   G6 (Gmaj6, Gmajor6, GM6)

1 - 3 - 5 - 6
G - B - D - E

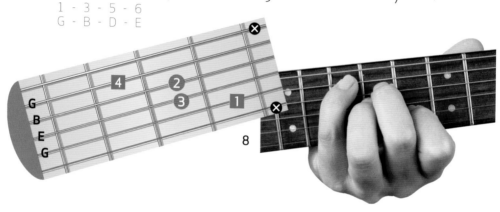

5   G6 (Gmaj6, Gmajor6, GM6)

1 - 3 - 5 - 6
G - B - D - E

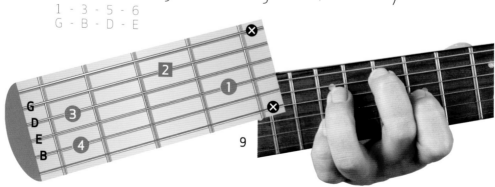

G MAJOR

The warm and jazzy major seventh chord is a firm favorite with jazz guitarists worldwide; it is also frequently used in more mainstream genres such as pop, rock, funk, and fusion, where it adds texture and depth, particularly when used as a sustained chord (e.g. Red Hot Chili Peppers' "Under The Bridge") or as a funky vamp chord (Bill Withers' "Lovely Day").

1 Gmaj7 (G△, Gmajor7, GM7)

1 - 3 - 5 - 7
G - B - D - F#

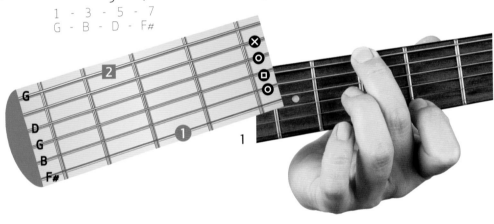

2 Gmaj7 (G△, Gmajor7, GM7)

1 - 3 - 5 - 7
G - B - D - F#

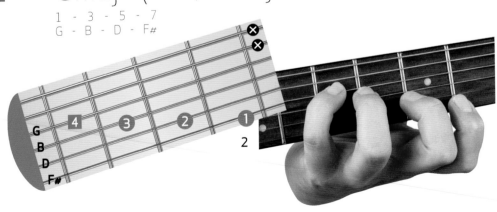

3 Gmaj7 (G△, Gmajor7, GM7)

1 - 3 - 5 - 7
G - B - D - F#

4 Gmaj7 (G△, Gmajor7, GM7)

1 - 3 - 5 - 7
G - B - D - F#

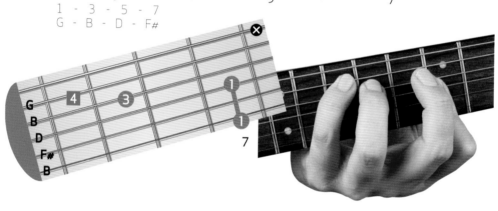

5 Gmaj7 (G△, Gmajor7, GM7)

1 - 3 - 5 - 7
G - B - D - F#

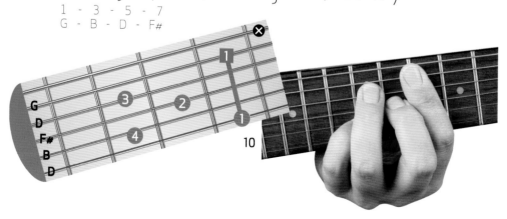

G

G MAJOR
Gsus (G suspended)

Suspended chords are traditionally used to "mask" the identity of a major chord. This creates tension that resolves when the chord is followed by a similar major voicing. However, in more contemporary styles, the suspended chord (especially the sus2) is used unresolved to create harmonic ambiguity. **Gsus2: 2** This works well followed by G major, shape 5 on page 141.

1 Gsus2

1 - 2 - 5
G - A - D

2 Gsus2

1 - 2 - 5
G - A - D

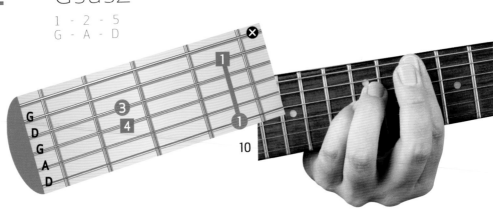

1 Gsus4

1 - 4 - 5
G - C - D

G

2 Gsus4

1 - 4 - 5
G - C - D

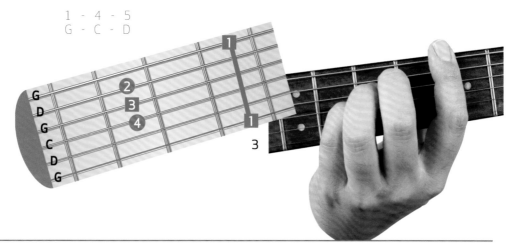

3 Gsus4

1 - 4 - 5
G - C - D

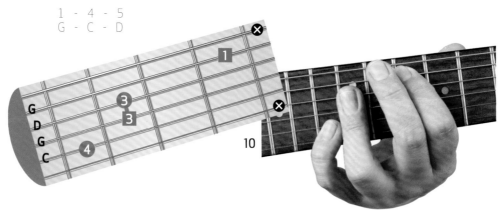

G MINOR

G minor is often described as the most melancholic of minor keys; for guitar players, the total absence of an open chord shape would suggest that it is a "guitar-unfriendly" key. However, being the relative minor of Bb major makes this a great key for horn players and so it frequently occurs in genres that feature horns (jazz, latin, soul, and funk).

1   GM (Gmin, Gminor, G−)

1 - b3 - 5
G - Bb - D

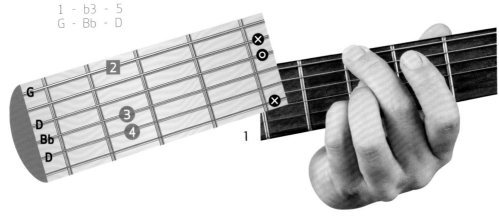

2   GM (Gmin, Gminor, G−)

1 - b3 - 5
G - Bb - D

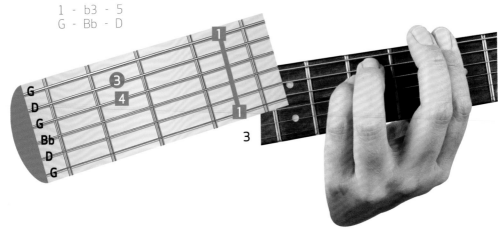

3 ## GM (Gmin, Gminor, G–)

1 – b3 – 5
G – Bb – D

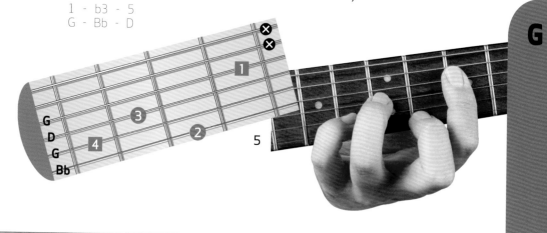

4 ## GM (Gmin, Gminor, G–)

1 – b3 – 5
G – Bb – D

5 ## GM (Gmin, Gminor, G–)

1 – b3 – 5
G – Bb – D

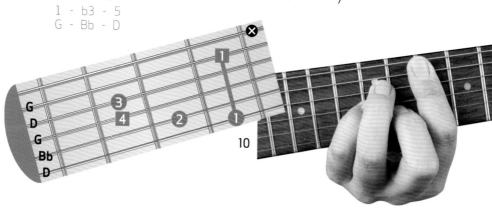

G

G MINOR

The minor sixth chord is a much darker sounding chord than its basic minor cousin; by way of contrast the minor seventh has a lighter, breezier texture that gives it a happy, optimistic quality.

Gmin6: 1 Low-register, deep voicing with a full sound.

Gmin7: 1 Six-string, full-sounding chord that is ideal for strummed chord rhythms.

1

Gmin6 (Gminor6, Gm6, G–6)

1 - b3 - 5 - 6
G - Bb - D - E

2

Gmin6 (Gminor6, Gm6, G–6)

1 - b3 - 5 - 6
G - Bb - D - E

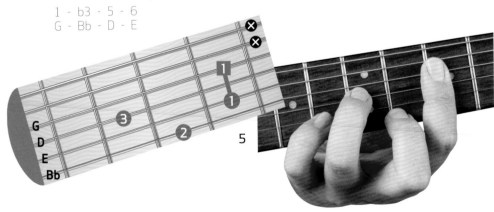

1 Gmin7 (Gminor7, Gm7, G–7)

1 - b3 - 5 - b7
G - Bb - D - F

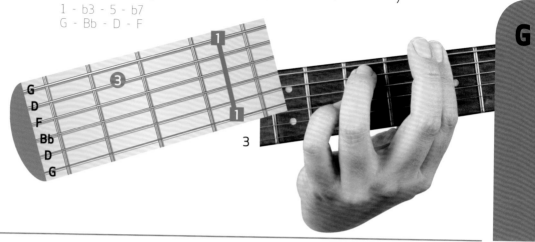

2 Gmin7 (Gminor7, Gm7, G–7)

1 - b3 - 5 - b7
G - Bb - D - F

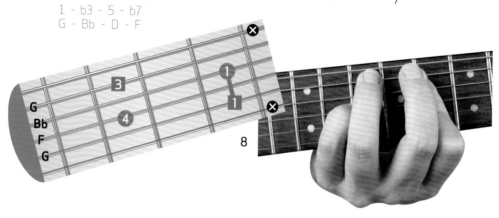

3 Gmin7 (Gminor7, Gm7, G–7)

1 - b3 - 5 - b7
G - Bb - D - F

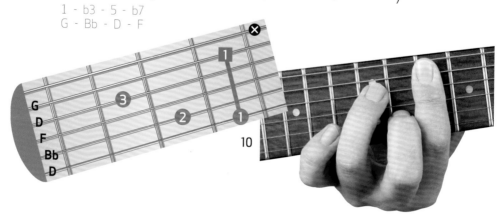

G

G7

Male vocalists love to sing the blues in G; consequently many famous blues songs have been written in this key. This is also a great key for fingerstyle blues since the three primary chords (G7, C7, and D7) are all playable as open shapes. **1** Six-string open voicing with a big sound—great for a quick change to an open C or C7 chord.

1 ## G7 (Gdom7)

1 - 3 - 5 - b7
G - B - D - F

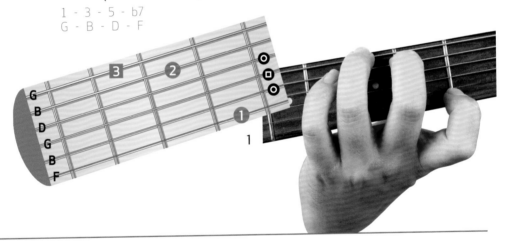

2 ## G7 (Gdom7)

1 - 3 - 5 - b7
G - B - D - F

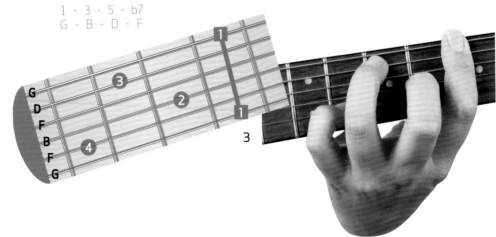

3   G7 (Gdom7)

1 - 3 - 5 - b7
G - B - D - F

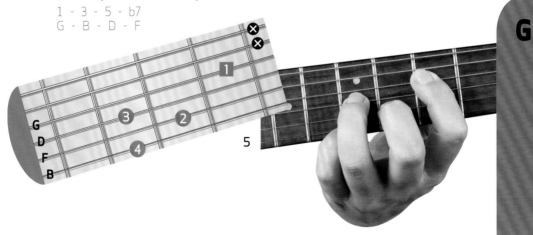

4   G7 (Gdom7)

1 - 3 - 5 - b7
G - B - D - F

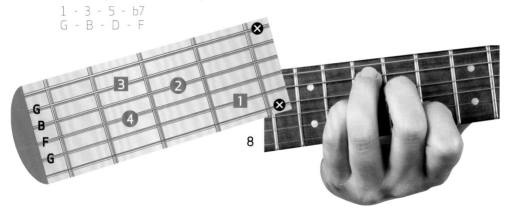

5   G7 (Gdom7)

1 - 3 - 5 - b7
G - B - D - F

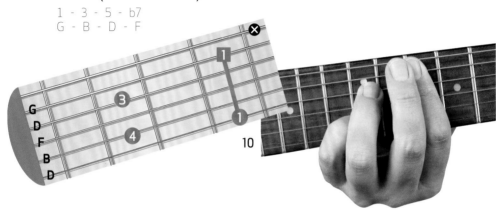

G

G7

Dominant seventh chords with a sharpened fifth are the ultimate perfect cadence chords (e.g. G7#5 to C) and really don't work too well as a static sound—they imply harmonic movement. By contrast, a suspended seventh chord also suggests movement but less dramatically than its sharpened fifth cousin, and so is frequently left unresolved to create static, ambiguous harmonic backdrops.

1 G7#5 (G7aug, G7+)

1 - 3 - #5 - b7
G - B - D# - F

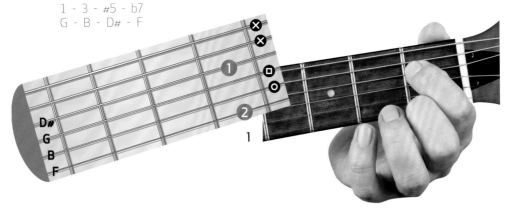

2 G7#5 (G7aug, G7+)

1 - 3 - #5 - b7
G - B - D# - F

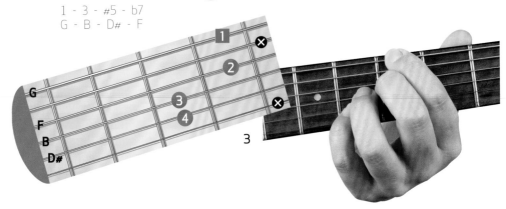

1   # G7sus (G7sus4)

1 - 4 - 5 - b7
G - C - D - F

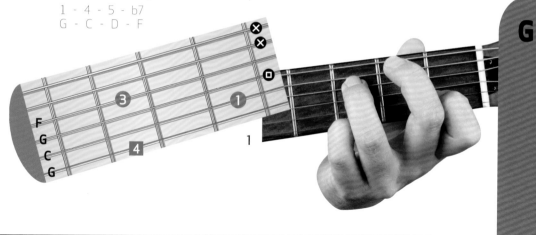

2   # G7sus (G7sus4)

1 - 4 - 5 - b7
G - C - D - F

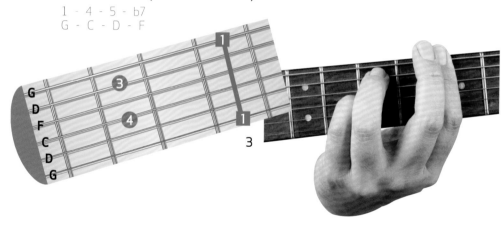

3   # G7sus (G7sus4)

1 - 4 - 5 - b7
G - C - D - F

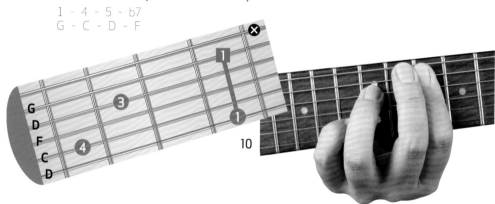

G

G 7

This selection of "spicy" dominant seventh chords are not just used for jazz, but also occur in many more "mainstream" genres and can be used to add a twist and extra depth to an otherwise predictable chord sequence.
G13: 1 This big, resonant chord gets its full sound from the two high open strings that contrast with the deep bass note on the sixth string.

G9 (Gdom9)

1 - 3 - 5 - b7 - 9
G - B - D - F - A

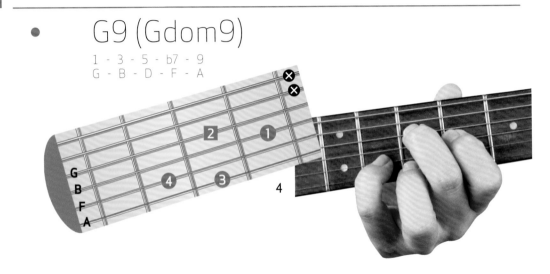

G7#9

1 - 3 - 5 - b7 - #9
G - B - D - F - A#

● G7b9

1 - 3 - 5 - b7 - b9
G - B - D - F - Ab

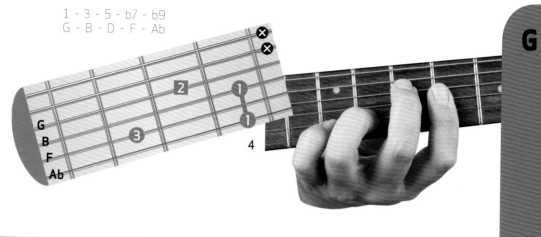

G

---

1 G13

1 - 3 - 5 - b7 - 9 - 13
G - B - D - F - A - E

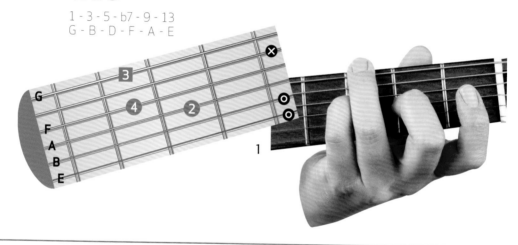

---

2 G13

1 - 3 - 5 - b7 - 9 - 13
G - B - D - F - A - E

Ab MAJOR

From a guitarist's perspective, Ab major has none of the resonance of E, A, or G major since only the seventh of the scale (G) can be played as an open string—consequently, there are no open chord shapes in this key. However, it should not be dismissed as an infrequently encountered key. Professional guitarists are equally proficient in every key; listen to ex-Steely Dan sideman Larry Carlton soloing effortlessly in Ab on "Don't Give It Up" (from his 1987 solo album *Last Nite*).

1 ## Ab (Abmaj, Abmajor, AbM)

1 - 3 - 5
Ab - C - Eb

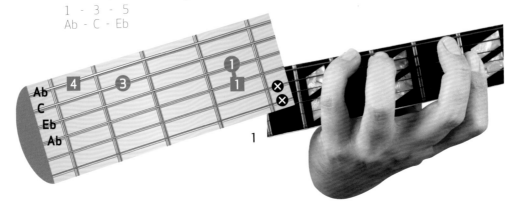

2 ## Ab (Abmaj, Abmajor, AbM)

1 - 3 - 5
Ab - C - Eb

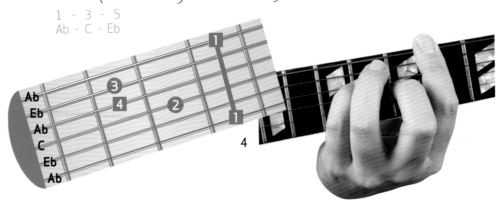

3 Ab (Abmaj, Abmajor, AbM)

1 - 3 - 5
Ab - C - Eb

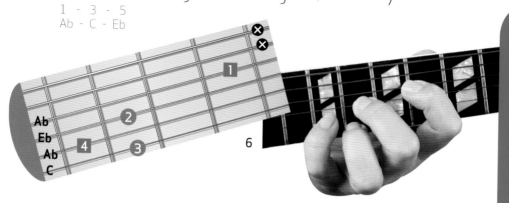

4 Ab (Abmaj, Abmajor, AbM)

1 - 3 - 5
Ab - C - Eb

5 Ab (Abmaj, Abmajor, AbM)

1 - 3 - 5
Ab - C - Eb

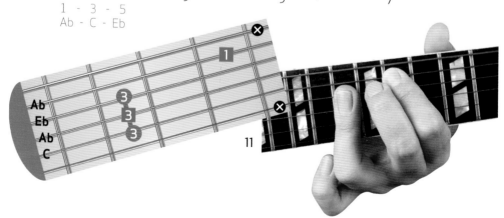

Ab MAJOR

Sixth chords are simply major chords with the interval of a sixth added for extra harmonic texture. To transform a basic Ab major chord to a "sixth," a single F note is added to the basic voicing. **3** Concise four-note shape with no doubled notes but the third raised an octave for a resonant sound. **5** This is an identical voicing to 3, but since it is played higher up the neck and on lower strings, it has a fuller sound.

1 ## Ab6 (Abmaj6, Abmajor6, AbM6)

1 - 3 - 5 - 6
Ab - C - Eb - F

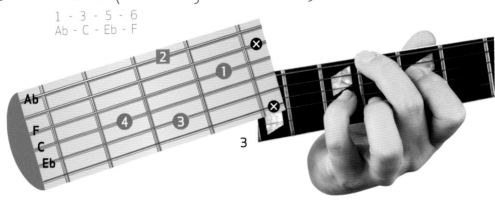

2 ## Ab6 (Abmaj6, Abmajor6, AbM6)

1 - 3 - 5 - 6
Ab - C - Eb - F

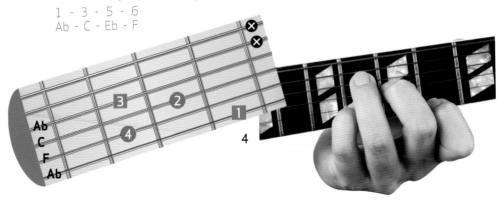

3   # Ab6 (Abmaj6, Abmajor6, AbM6)

1 - 3 - 5 - 6
Ab - C - Eb - F

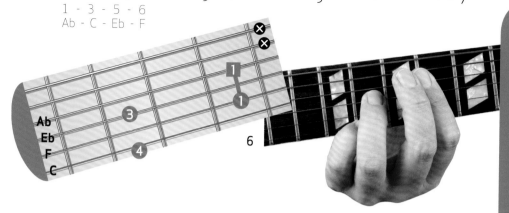

4   # Ab6 (Abmaj6, Abmajor6, AbM6)

1 - 3 - 5 - 6
Ab - C - Eb - F

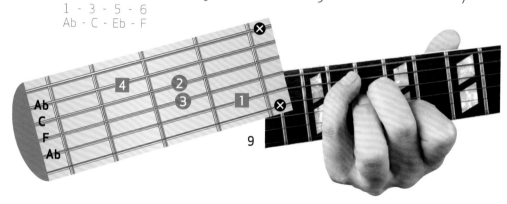

5   # Ab6 (Abmaj6, Abmajor6, AbM6)

1 - 3 - 5 - 6
Ab - C - Eb - F

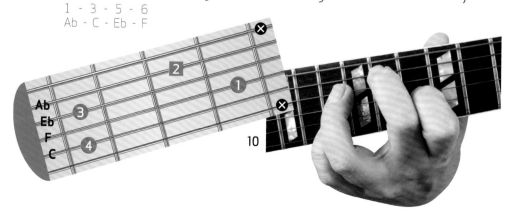

Ab MAJOR

Major seventh chords play a big part in the bossa nova sound that was created by the legendary composer Antonio Carlos Jobim in the early '60s. The "summery" sound of these chords is perfect for the subtle rhythms and jazzy textures of a style with Latin-American roots. With melodies frequently featuring horn players, Ab is a common key for this genre.

1 Abmaj7 (Ab△, Abmajor7, AbM7)

1 - 3 - 5 - 7
Ab - C - Eb - G

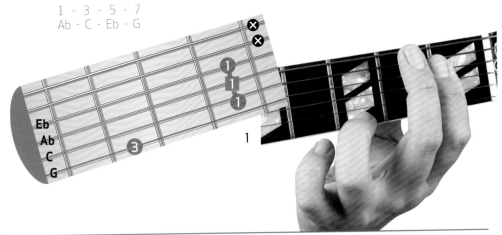

2 Abmaj7 (Ab△, Abmajor7, AbM7)

1 - 3 - 5 - 7
Ab - C - Eb - G

3 Abmaj7 (Ab△, Abmajor7, AbM7)

1 - 3 - 5 - 7
Ab - C - Eb - G

4 Abmaj7 (Ab△, Abmajor7, AbM7)

1 - 3 - 5 - 7
Ab - C - Eb - G

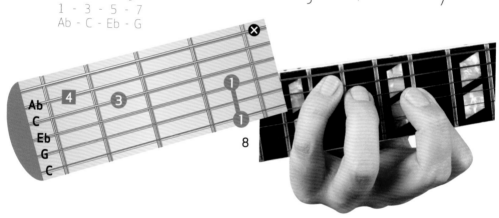

5 Abmaj7 (Ab△, Abmajor7, AbM7)

1 - 3 - 5 - 7
Ab - C - Eb - G

Ab

Ab MAJOR
Absus (Ab suspended)

Composers frequently use suspended chords to create harmonic ambiguity since the addition of the second (Bb) or fourth (Db) "suspends" the third of the chord and disguises its tonality.

Absus2: 1 A high-register, four-note voicing with the second as the top voice of the chord.

Absus4: 1 Unusual four-string inversion with the fifth in the bass.

---

1   Absus2

1 - 2 - 5
Ab - Bb - Eb

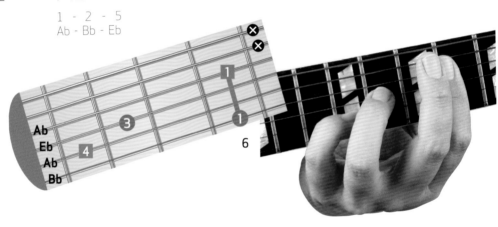

2   Absus2

1 - 2 - 5
Ab - Bb - Eb

1 Absus4

1 - 4 - 5
Ab - Db - Eb

2 Absus4

1 - 4 - 5
Ab - Db - Eb

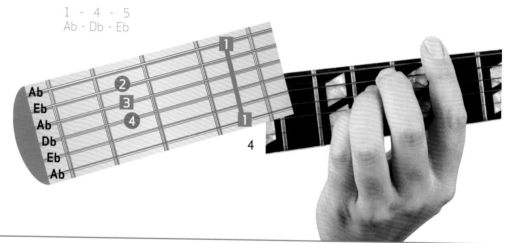

3 Absus4

1 - 4 - 5
Ab - Db - Eb

Ab

Ab MINOR

The key of Ab minor has a key signature containing seven flats, as it is the relative minor key of Cb major and this makes it an unlikely guitar key. However, the chord of Ab minor could easily be encountered as a passing chord or as a temporary modulation within a song so it is well worth familiarizing yourself with these voicings.

1 ## Abm (Abmin, Abminor, Ab–)

1 - b3 - 5
Ab - Cb - Eb

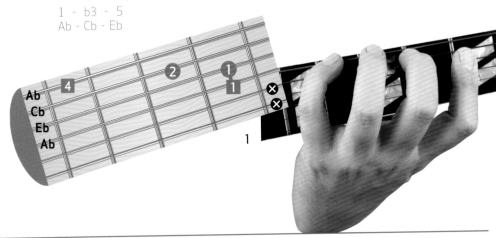

2 ## Abm (Abmin, Abminor, Ab–)

1 - b3 - 5
Ab - Cb - Eb

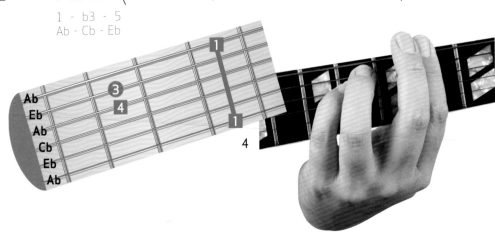

3 Abm (Abmin, Abminor, Ab-)

1 - b3 - 5
Ab - Cb - Eb

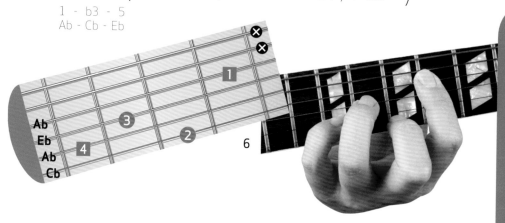

4 Abm (Abmin, Abminor, Ab-)

1 - b3 - 5
Ab - Cb - Eb

5 Abm (Abmin, Abminor, Ab-)

1 - b3 - 5
Ab - Cb - Eb

Ab MINOR

A great way to "spice up" a basic Ab minor chord is to add the sixth (F) or the flattened seventh (Gb).

Abmin6: 2 A four-note, mid-register voicing with the third raised an octave —ideal for syncopated funk rhythms.

Abmin7: 2 A simple four-note chord containing a doubled root but no fifth, ideal for arpeggiated chord sequences.

1 ## Abmin6 (Abminor6, Abm6, Ab–6)

1 - b3 - 5 - 6
Ab - Cb - Eb - F

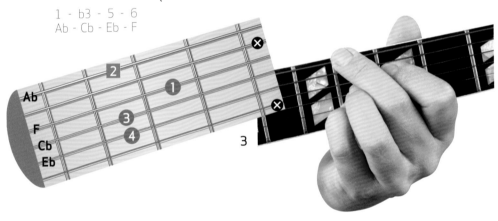

2 ## Abmin6 (Abminor6, Abm6, Ab–6)

1 - b3 - 5 - 6
Ab - Cb - Eb - F

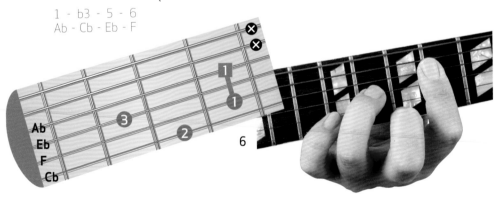

1 Abmin7 (Abminor7, Abm7, Ab–7)

1 - b3 - 5 - b7
Ab - Cb - Eb - Gb

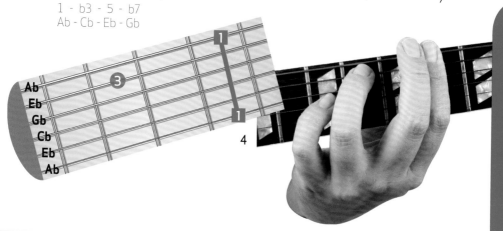

2 Abmin7 (Abminor7, Abm7, Ab–7)

1 - b3 - 5 - b7
Ab - Cb - Eb - Gb

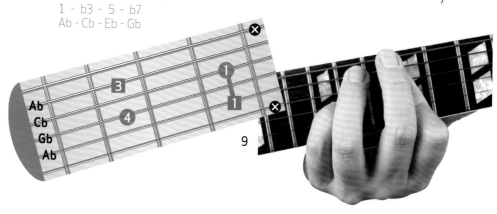

3 Abmin7 (Abminor7, Abm7, Ab–7)

1 - b3 - 5 - b7
Ab - Cb - Eb - Gb

Ab

Ab7

Although you are unlikely to encounter a blues in Ab, a blues in the key of Eb is fairly common, particularly in jazz and funk styles. Since Ab7 is the second chord of an Eb blues, there is a good chance you will need at least one of these five handy shapes at some point.

1   Ab7 (Abdom7)

1 - 3 - 5 - b7
Ab - C - Eb - Gb

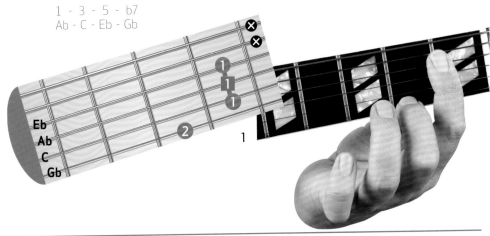

2   Ab7 (Abdom7)

1 - 3 - 5 - b7
Ab - C - Eb - Gb

3   ## Ab7 (Abdom7)

1 - 3 - 5 - b7
Ab - C - Eb - Gb

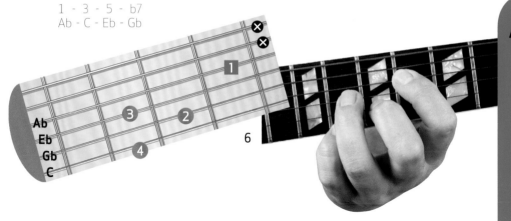

4   ## Ab7 (Abdom7)

1 - 3 - 5 - b7
Ab - C - Eb - Gb

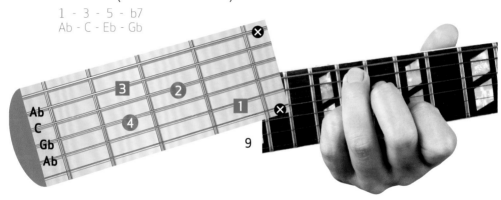

5   ## Ab7 (Abdom7)

1 - 3 - 5 - b7
Ab - C - Eb - Gb

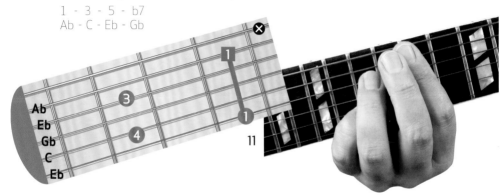

Ab

Ab7

These two types of seventh chord not only sound different but also perform very different musical tasks. Adding a sharpened fifth to a dominant seventh chord heightens the "pull" back to the home chord in a perfect (V–I) cadence. A suspended dominant seventh chord has a more static quality and can be alternated with its related seventh shape to create harmonic movement, e.g. a repetition of Ab7 could be replaced by Ab7sus - Ab7 - Ab7sus - Ab7.

1 ## Ab7#5 (Ab7aug, Ab7+)

1 - 3 - #5 - b7
Ab - C - E - Gb

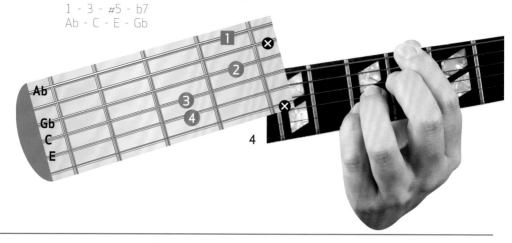

2 ## Ab7#5 (Ab7aug, Ab7+)

1 - 3 - #5 - b7
Ab - C - E - Gb

1   Ab7sus (Ab7sus4)

1 - 3 - 5 - b7
Ab - Db - Eb - Gb

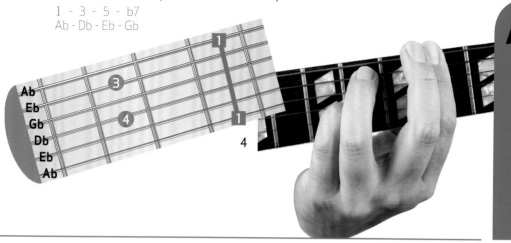

2   Ab7sus (Ab7sus4)

1 - 3 - 5 - b7
Ab - Db - Eb - Gb

3   Ab7sus (Ab7sus4)

1 - 3 - 5 - b7
Ab - Db - Eb - Gb

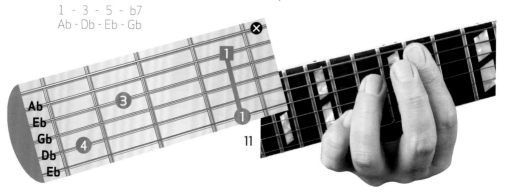

Ab7

Ninth and thirteenth chords are often wrongly assumed to have been "invented" by jazz musicians. However, during the Impressionist movement of the late nineteenth century, the classical composer Claude Debussy frequently incorporated dominant ninth and thirteenth chords in his work. These new sounds were also sometimes left "unresolved" exactly as they would be in the blues and jazz that followed in the twentieth century.

- ## Ab9 (Abdom9)
  1 - 3 - 5 - b7 - 9
  Ab - C - Eb - Gb - Bb

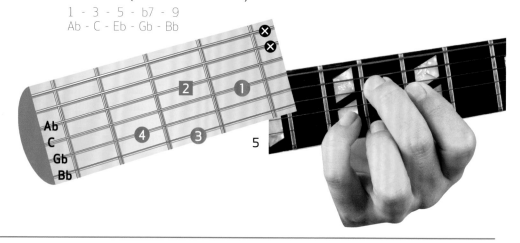

- ## Ab7#9
  1 - 3 - 5 - b7 - #9
  Ab - C - Eb - Gb - B

● ## Ab7b9

1 - 3 - 5 - b7 - b9
Ab - C - Eb - Gb - Bbb

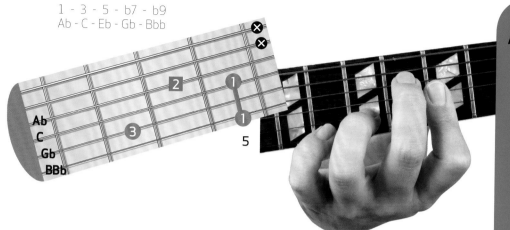

1 ## Ab13

1 - 3 - 5 - b7 - 9 - 13
Ab - C - Eb - Gb - Bb - F

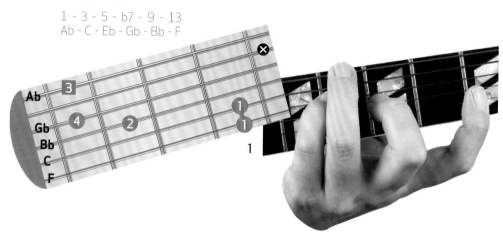

2 ## Ab13

1 - 3 - 5 - b7 - 9 - 13
Ab - C - Eb - Gb - Bb - F

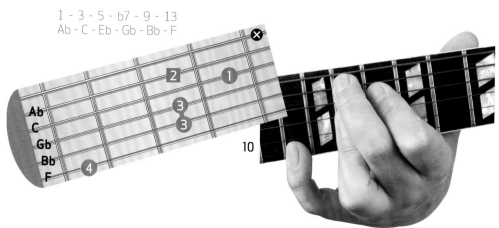

A MAJOR

A major is a very "guitar-friendly" key; not only are most of the open strings notes within the A major scale, but also the three primary chords (A, D, and E) are all open chord shapes. **1** Classic open, five-string voicing with doubled root and fifth. **2** A variation on the previous shape that replaces the doubled fifth with a high root note creating a more "open" sound.

1 A (Amaj, Amajor, AM)

1 - 3 - 5
A - C# - E

2 A (Amaj, Amajor, AM)

1 - 3 - 5
A - C# - E

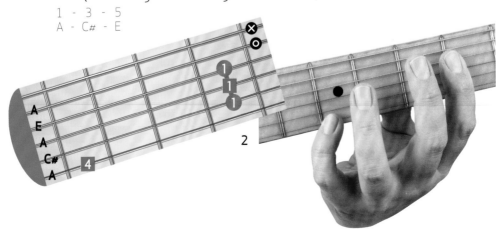

3 A (Amaj, Amajor, AM)

1 - 3 - 5
A - C# - E

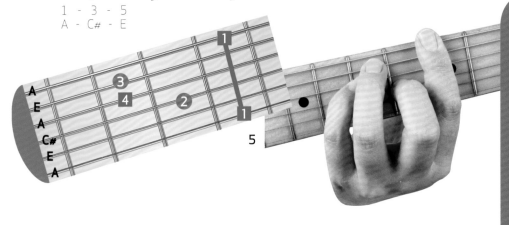

4 A (Amaj, Amajor, AM)

1 - 3 - 5
A - C# - E

5 A (Amaj, Amajor, AM)

1 - 3 - 5
A - C# - E

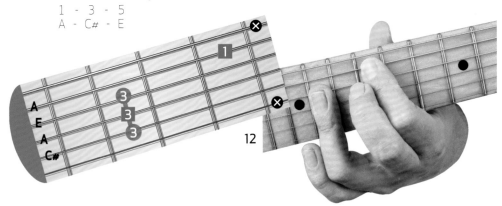

A MAJOR

The sixth chord has been used in every style from rockabilly to jazz as a final cadence (ending) chord. **2** The inclusion of the open root note on the fifth string adds extra depth to this mid-register voicing. **5** Versatile four-note voicing with a raised third and a solid "root plus fifth" power chord foundation.

1 A6 (Amaj6, Amajor6, AM6)
1 - 3 - 5 - 6
A - C# - E - F#

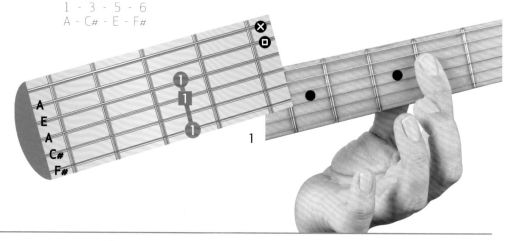

2 A6 (Amaj6, Amajor6, AM6)
1 - 3 - 5 - 6
A - C# - E - F#

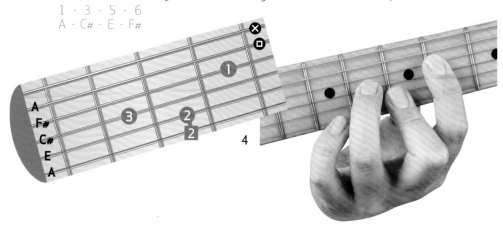

3   A6 (Amaj6, Amajor6, AM6)

1 - 3 - 5 - 6
A - C# - E - F#

A

4   A6 (Amaj6, Amajor6, AM6)

1 - 3 - 5 - 6
A - C# - E - F#

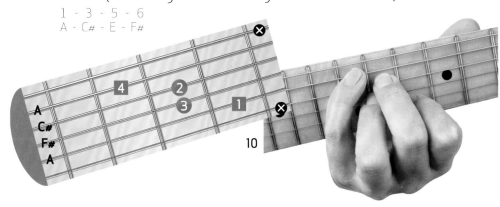

5   A6 (Amaj6, Amajor6, AM6)

1 - 3 - 5 - 6
A - C# - E - F#

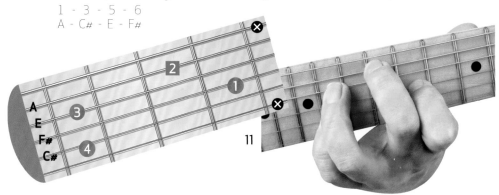

A MAJOR

The major seventh is arguably the jazziest and coolest of all the major chords, though it's not just for jazz but is used in many other styles. For a brilliant example of usage within the rock genre, listen to the verse section of Jimi Hendrix's "Castles Made of Sand" from his outstanding 1967 album *Axis: Bold as Love*.

1
Amaj7 (A△, Amajor7, AM7)

1 - 3 - 5 - 7
A - C# - E - G#

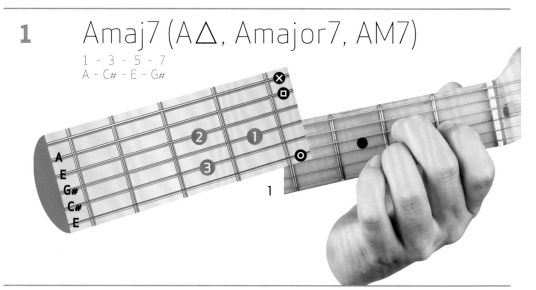

2
Amaj7 (A△, Amajor7, AM7)

1 - 3 - 5 - 7
A - C# - E - G#

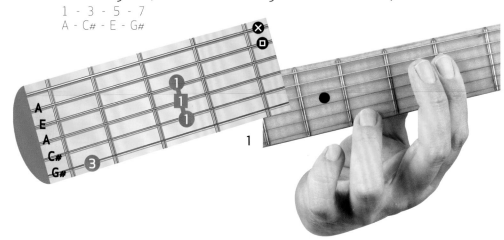

3 Amaj7 (A△, Amajor7, AM7)

1 - 3 - 5 - 7
A - C# - E - G#

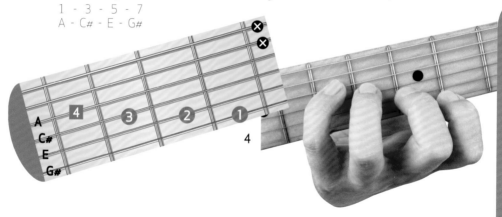

4 Amaj7 (A△, Amajor7, AM7)

1 - 3 - 5 - 7
A - C# - E - G#

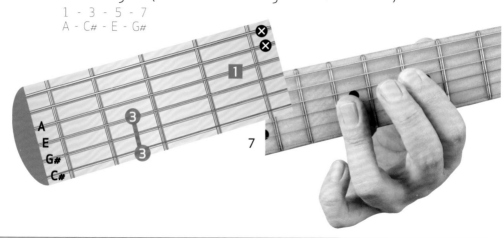

5 Amaj7 (A△, Amajor7, AM7)

1 - 3 - 5 - 7
A - C# - E - G#

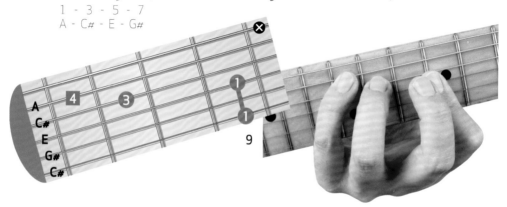

A MAJOR
Asus (A suspended)

Asus2: 1 Exclusive to the key of A, this five-string shape is perfect for country-flavored guitar—try "hammering-on" the C# (fret 2, string 2) for a fantastic pedal-steel simulation.
Asus4: 1 Resonant open chord with doubled root and fifth that also resolves perfectly to A major, shape 1 on page 176.

1 Asus2

1 - 2 - 5
A - B - E

2 Asus2

1 - 2 - 5
A - B - E

1 # Asus4
1 - 4 - 5
A - D - E

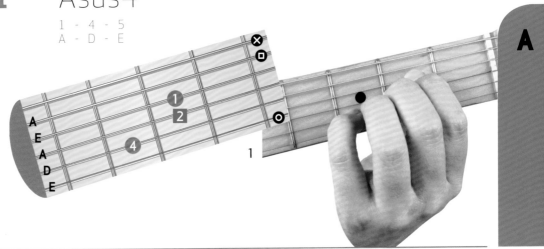

2 # Asus4
1 - 4 - 5
A - D - E

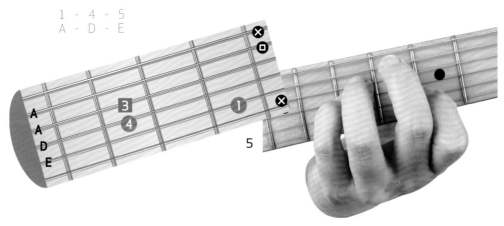

3 # Asus4
1 - 4 - 5
A - D - E

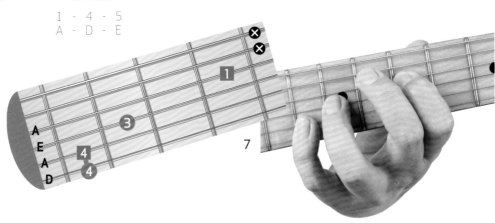

A

A MINOR

The characteristics of the key of A minor have been described as "simple, naïve, sad, and rustic"—qualities that perfectly describe Beethoven's "Für Elise" written in Am. They could also be used to describe The Animals' version of the folk standard, "House of the Rising Sun," with its hypnotic cyclic Am chord sequence in 12/8 time.

1 Am (Amin, Aminor, A–)

1 - b3 - 5
A - C - E

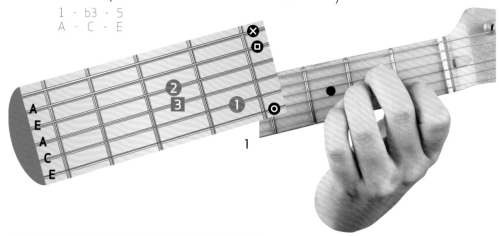

2 Am (Amin, Aminor, A–)

1 - b3 - 5
A - C - E

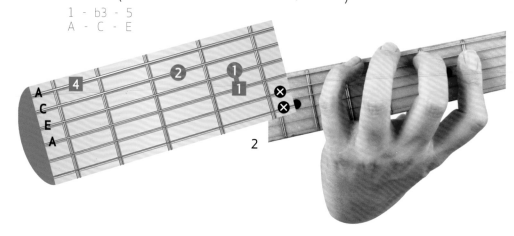

3 Am (Amin, Aminor, A–)

1 - b3 - 5
A - C - E

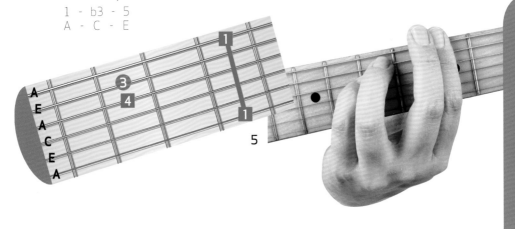

4 Am (Amin, Aminor, A–)

1 - b3 - 5
A - C - E

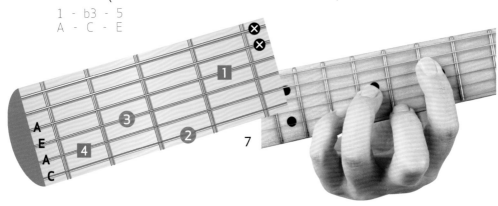

5 Am (Amin, Aminor, A–)

1 - b3 - 5
A - C - E

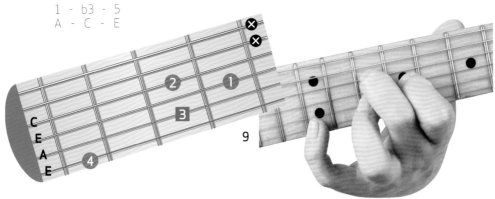

A MINOR

Sometimes a basic minor chord just doesn't add enough "color"—can you imagine Monty Norman's atmospheric James Bond Theme without the classic accompaniment featuring minor sixth chords? Similarly, the Doobie Brothers' 70's classic "Long Train Runnin'" opens with a distinctive minor seventh vamp that just wouldn't work if it had been based on a straight minor chord.

1 Amin6 (Aminor6, Am6, A–6)

1 - b3 - 5 - 6
A - C - E - F#

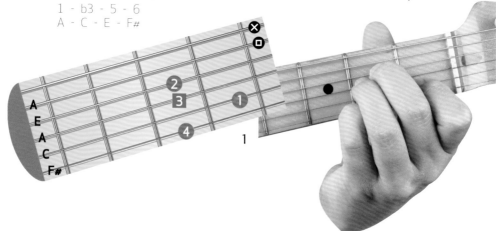

2 Amin6 (Aminor6, Am6, A–6)

1 - b3 - 5 - 6
A - C - E - F#

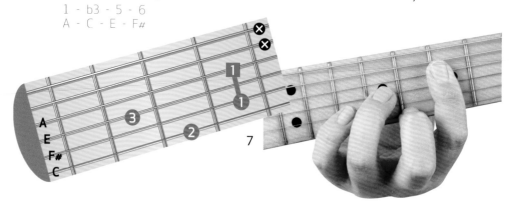

1 Amin7 (Aminor7, Am7, A−7)

1 - b3 - 5 - b7
A - C - E - G

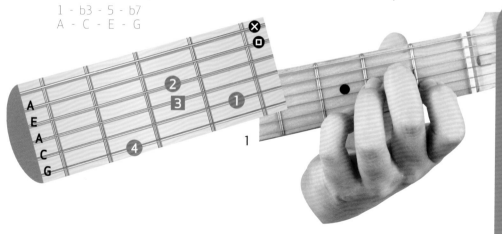

A

2 Amin7 (Aminor7, Am7, A−7)

1 - b3 - 5 - b7
A - C - E - G

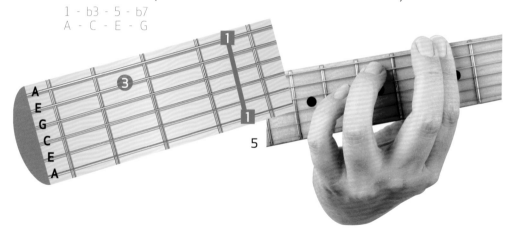

3 Amin7 (Aminor7, Am7, A−7)

1 - b3 - 5 - b7
A - C - E - G

A7

Since A major is one of the commonest keys for guitar-led blues, these five A7 shapes really are essential for any self-respecting blues player. For a brilliant example of how good blues-rock can sound in this key, listen to Jimmy Page's blistering riffs and use of seventh chords in Led Zeppelin's classic "Rock and Roll" from their untitled fourth album.

1 A7 (Adom7)

1 - 3 - 5 - b7
A - C# - E - G

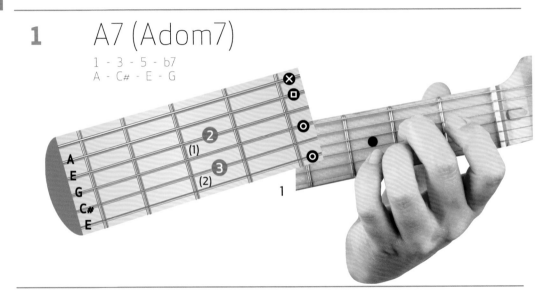

2 A7 (Adom7)

1 - 3 - 5 - b7
A - C# - E - G

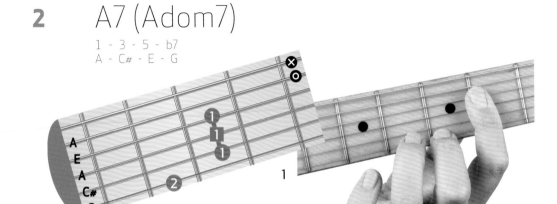

3

A7 (Adom7)

1 - 3 - 5 - b7
A - C# - E - G

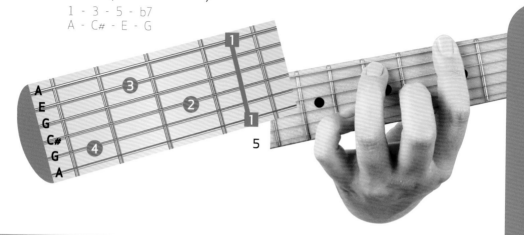

A

4

A7 (Adom7)

1 - 3 - 5 - b7
A - C# - E - G

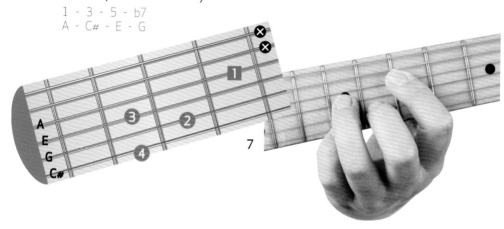

5

A7 (Adom7)

1 - 3 - 5 - b7
A - C# - E - G

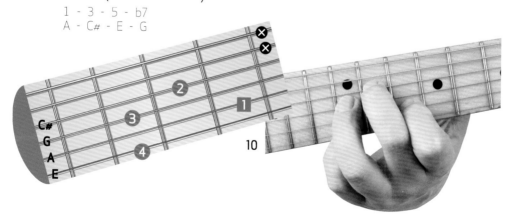

A

A7

Below are two very useful dominant sevenths with the fifth of the chord sharpened—commonly described as "sharp five" seventh chords. The sharpened fifth is seldom doubled (unlike the natural fifth) since it has such a strong sound. On the page opposite there are three "suspended seventh" voicings— these chords are often simply referred to as "seventh sus" chords, since a suspended second dominant seventh is an anomaly.

1 A7#5 (A7aug, A7+)

1 - 3 - #5 - b7
A - C# - E# - G

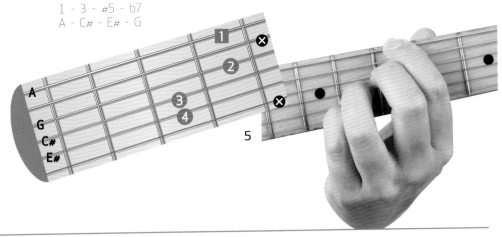

2 A7#5 (A7aug, A7+)

1 - 3 - #5 - b7
A - C# - E# - G

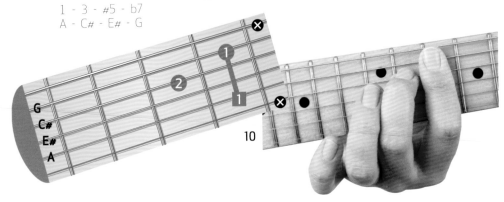

1 A7sus (A7sus4)

1 - 4 - 5 - b7
A - D - E - G

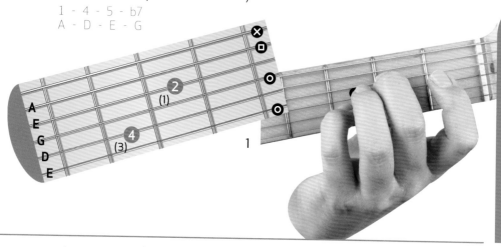

A

2 A7sus (A7sus4)

1 - 4 - 5 - b7
A - D - E - G

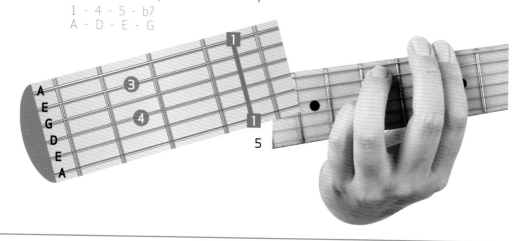

3 A7sus (A7sus4)

1 - 4 - 5 - b7
A - D - E - G

A

A7

Here are five dominant sevenths with either the ninth or thirteenth (often also including the ninth) added; these are "color tones" that are added to a basic seventh chord to create additional harmonic interest.
A9 Versatile four-note ninth voicing with a bright and breezy sound.
A13: 1 The inclusion of the open root note on the fifth string adds weight to this complex five-string chord.

A9 (Adom9)

1 - 3 - 5 - b7 - 9
A - C# - E - G - B

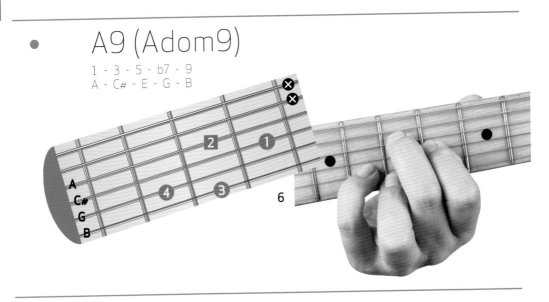

A7#9

1 - 3 - 5 - b7 - #9
A - C# - E - G - B#

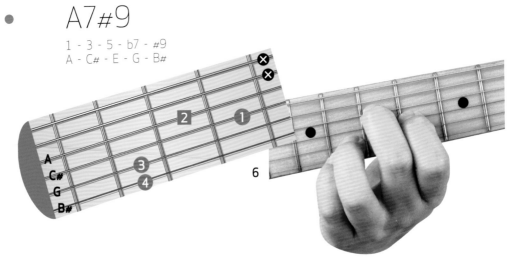

A7b9

1 - 3 - 5 - b7 - b9
A - C# - E - G - Bb

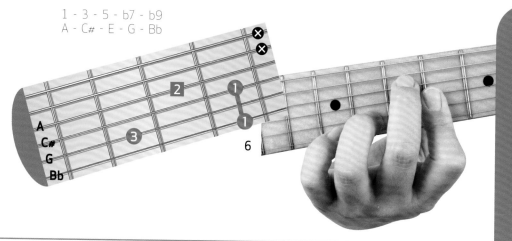

1 A13

1 - 3 - 5 - b7 - 9 - 13
A - C# - E - G - B - F#

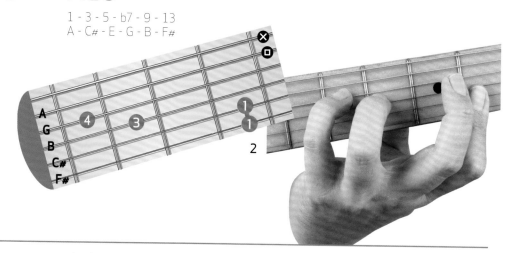

2 A13

1 - 3 - 5 - b7 - 9 - 13
A - C# - E - G - B - F#

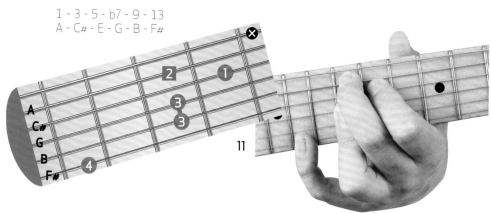

Bb

Bb MAJOR

Horn players (saxophone, trumpet, and trombone) love the key of Bb. So you are most likely going to need to use this key when playing in styles that feature these instruments (e.g. jazz, Chicago blues, soul, and funk). **1** The lowest shape on the guitar neck in this key is in second position with its root on the fifth string.

1 Bb (Bbmaj, Bbmajor, BbM)

1 - 3 - 5
Bb - D - F

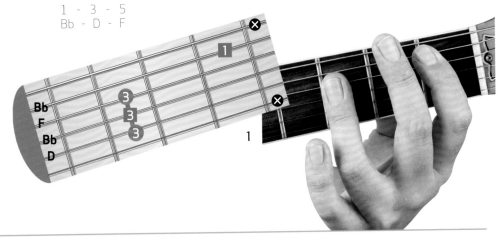

2 Bb (Bbmaj, Bbmajor, BbM)

1 - 3 - 5
Bb - D - F

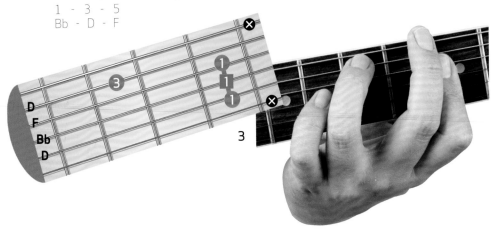

3

Bb (Bbmaj, Bbmajor, BbM)

1 - 3 - 5
Bb - D - F

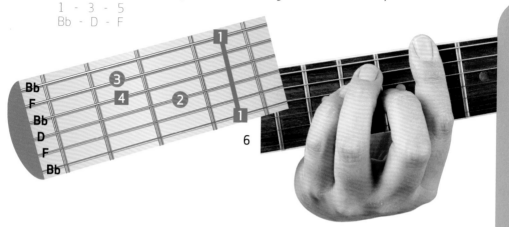

4

Bb (Bbmaj, Bbmajor, BbM)

1 - 3 - 5
Bb - D - F

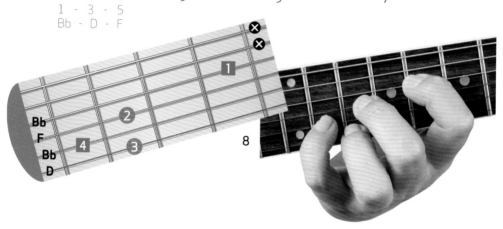

5

Bb (Bbmaj, Bbmajor, BbM)

1 - 3 - 5
Bb - D - F

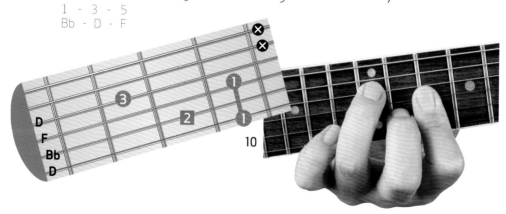

Bb MAJOR

Playing the blues in Bb is extremely common in the jazz world and often "freaks out" the novice guitarist who would probably be more comfortable playing in A just a half-step (one fret) away. George Gershwin's "I Got Rhythm" is one of the most frequently used chord sequences in jazz (usually with an original melody as in Charlie Parker's "Anthropology") and is normally played in Bb with the first chord played as Bb6.

1 Bb6 (Bbmaj6, Bbmajor6, BbM6)

1 - 3 - 5 - 6
Bb - D - F - G

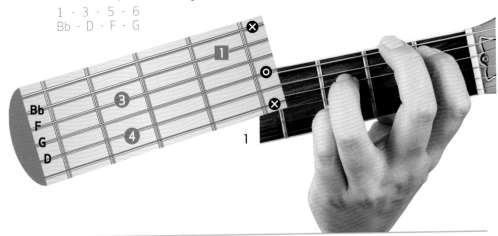

2 Bb6 (Bbmaj6, Bbmajor6, BbM6)

1 - 3 - 5 - 6
Bb - D - F - G

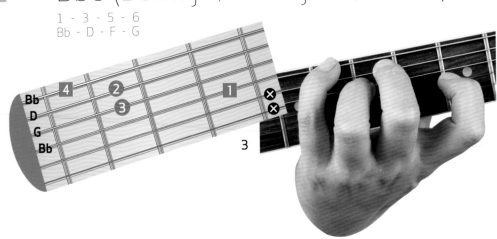

3

Bb6 (Bbmaj6, Bbmajor6, BbM6)

1 - 3 - 5 - 6
Bb - D - F - G

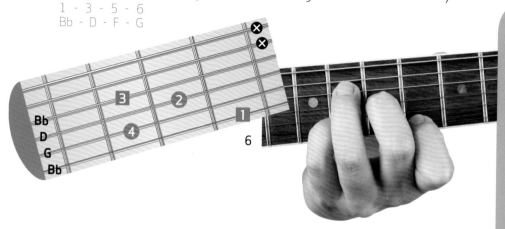

4

Bb6 (Bbmaj6, Bbmajor6, BbM6)

1 - 3 - 5 - 6
Bb - D - F - G

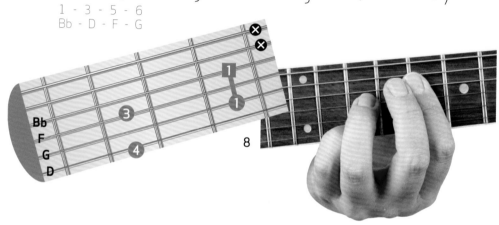

5

Bb6 (Bbmaj6, Bbmajor6, BbM6)

1 - 3 - 5 - 6
Bb - D - F - G

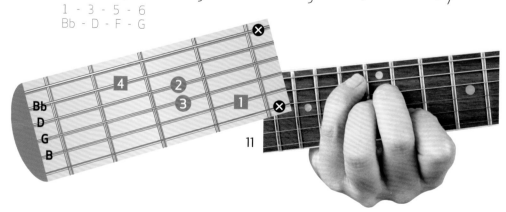

Bb MAJOR

Since the key of Bb is predominantly used in jazz, and the major seventh is used more widely than a straight major chord in the genre, these five shapes are absolutely essential stuff for the aspiring jazz guitarist. **1** The lowest shape of Bbmaj7 is at the first fret. **3** Sweet and light-sounding, "closed" piano-style voicing—great for post-bop style comping.

1 ## Bbmaj7 (Bb△, Bbmajor7, BbM7)
1 - 3 - 5 - 7
Bb - D - F - A

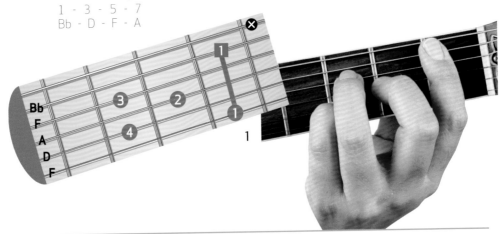

2 ## Bbmaj7 (Bb△, Bbmajor7, BbM7)
1 - 3 - 5 - 7
Bb - D - F - A

3

Bbmaj7 (Bb△, Bbmajor7, BbM7)

1 - 3 - 5 - 7
Bb - D - F - A

Bb

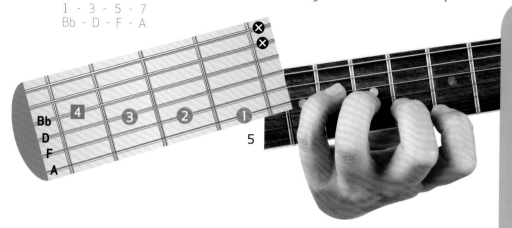

4

Bbmaj7 (Bb△, Bbmajor7, BbM7)

1 - 3 - 5 - 7
Bb - D - F - A

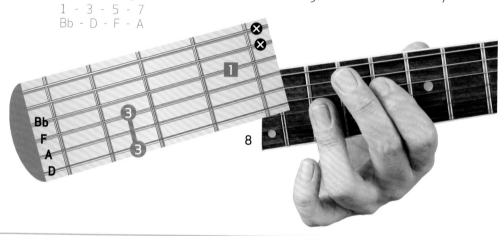

5

Bbmaj7 (Bb△, Bbmajor7, BbM7)

1 - 3 - 5 - 7
Bb - D - F - A

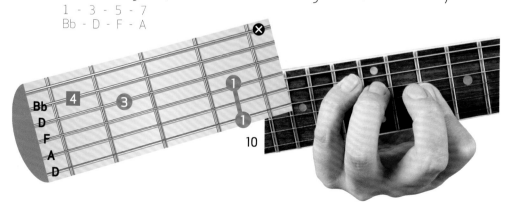

Bb MAJOR
Bbsus (Bb suspended)

Suspended chords are frequently used in ballads and slow tempo tunes where additional harmonic movement may be required. **Bbsus2: 1 and Bbsus4: 1** Experiment by substituting a whole bar of Bb major for one beat on these chords; arpeggiating the chords with a pick or fingerstyle will sound cool too.

1 Bbsus2

1 - 2 - 5
Bb - C - F

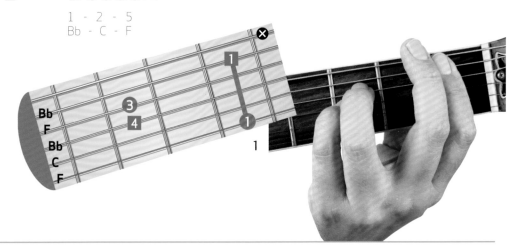

2 Bbsus2

1 - 2 - 5
Bb - C - F

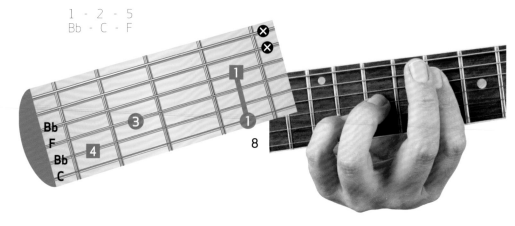

1   Bbsus4

1 - 4 - 5
Bb - Eb - F

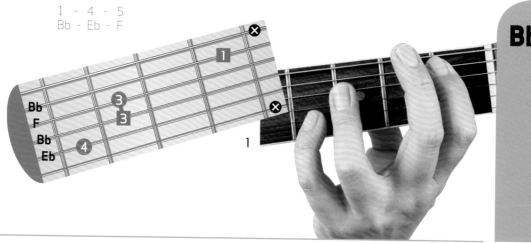

2   Bbsus4

1 - 4 - 5
Bb - Eb - F

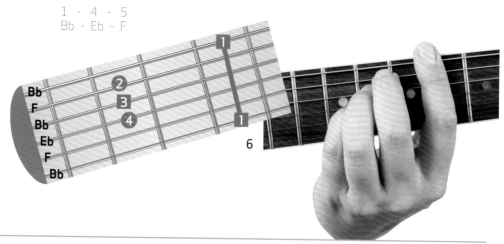

3   Bbsus4

1 - 4 - 5
Bb - Eb - F

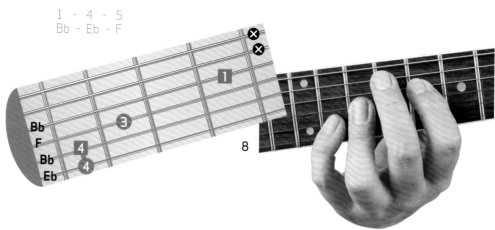

Bb MINOR

Bb minor is the relative minor of Db major and shares the same key signature containing five flats. It is infrequently encountered in rock and pop music due to the lack of open chord shapes in this key. However, it is used widely in genres dominated by horns and/or horn sections such as jazz, soul, and funk.
3 Full six-string minor shape with a big, resonant sound.

1

Bbm (Bbmin, Bbminor, Bb–)

1 - b3 - 5
Bb - Db - F

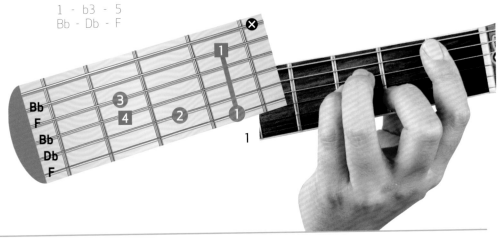

2

Bbm (Bbmin, Bbminor, Bb–)

1 - b3 - 5
Bb - Db - F

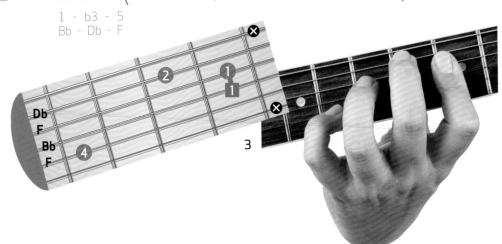

3

Bbm (Bbmin, Bbminor, Bb–)

1 - b3 - 5
Bb - Db - F

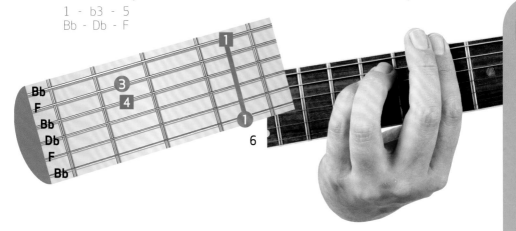

Bb

4

Bbm (Bbmin, Bbminor, Bb–)

1 - b3 - 5
Bb - Db - F

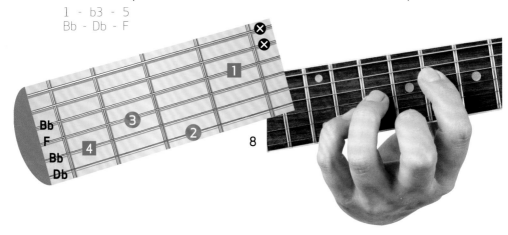

5

Bbm (Bbmin, Bbminor, Bb–)

1 - b3 - 5
Bb - Db - F

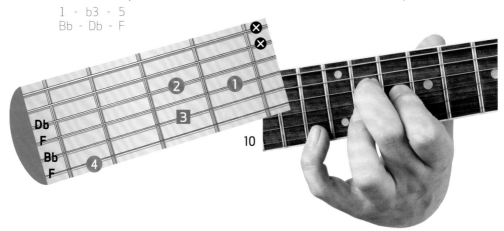

Bb MINOR

The major sixth and minor seventh intervals are frequently used to change the quality of a minor chord. A straight Bbm chord has a sad but fairly plain sound; adding the sixth makes the chord sound darker and more ominous, while the minor seventh transforms it into a lighter, jazzy-sounding chord.

1 ## Bbmin6 (Bbminor6, Bbm6, Bb–6)

1 - b3 - 5 - 6
Bb - Db - F - G

2 ## Bbmin6 (Bbminor6, Bbm6, Bb–6)

1 - b3 - 5 - 6
Bb - Db - F - G

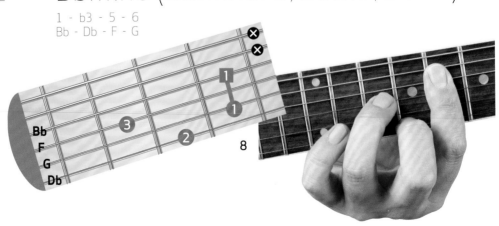

1 ## Bbmin7 (Bbminor7, Bbm7, Bb–7)

1 - b3 - 5 - b7
Bb - Db - F - Ab

2 ## Bbmin7 (Bbminor7, Bbm7, Bb–7)

1 - b3 - 5 - b7
Bb - Db - F - Ab

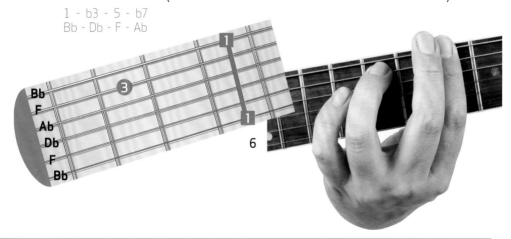

3 ## Bbmin7 (Bbminor7, Bbm7, Bb–7)

1 - b3 - 5 - b7
Bb - Db - F - Ab

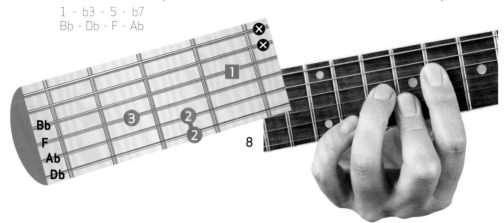

Bb7

You are most likely to encounter the Bb7 chord in one of two musical situations: as the tonic chord in a Bb7 blues, or as the dominant chord in the key of Eb. **2** A high-register chord played quite low on the neck that's great for syncopated rhythm work. **5** This high-register, four-note voicing is great for "chips" rhythm playing or when you need extra bite to cut through the rhythm section.

1

Bb7 (Bbdom7)

1 - 3 - 5 - b7
Bb - D - F - Ab

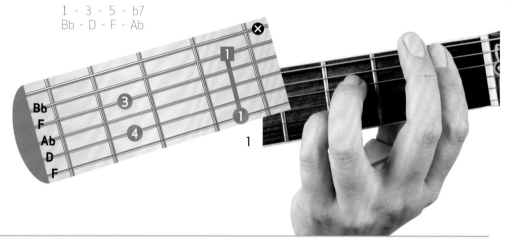

2

Bb7 (Bbdom7)

1 - 3 - 5 - b7
Bb - D - F - Ab

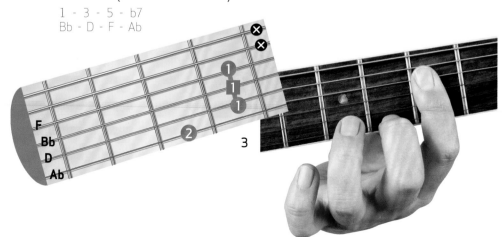

3   Bb7 (Bbdom7)

1 - 3 - 5 - b7
Bb - D - F - Ab

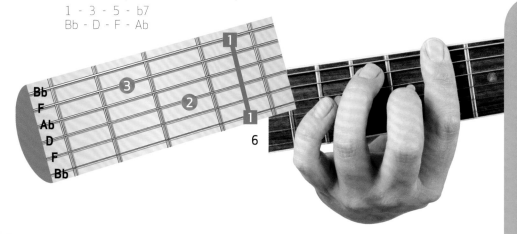

Bb

4   Bb7 (Bbdom7)

1 - 3 - 5 - b7
Bb - D - F - Ab

5   Bb7 (Bbdom7)

1 - 3 - 5 - b7
Bb - D - F - Ab

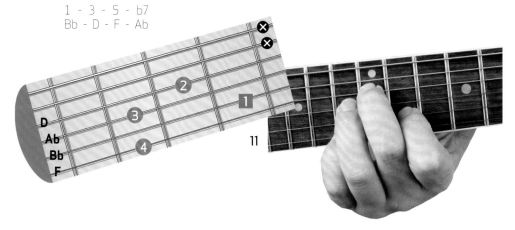

Bb

Bb7

The Bb7#5 chord has a very "dark" sound that can be used to heighten harmonic tension in a V (Bb7#5) to I (Eb/Ebm) perfect cadence. Suspended seventh chords can also be used to "spice up" a perfect cadence but in a different way: by creating additional harmonic movement within a V–I resolution (e.g. Bb7sus - Bb7 - Bb). This works well in ballads or mid to slow tempo tunes.

1 Bb7#5 (Bb7aug, Bb7+)

1 - 3 - #5 - b7
Bb - D - F# - Ab

2 Bb7#5 (Bb7aug, Bb7+)

1 - 3 - #5 - b7
Bb - D - F# - Ab

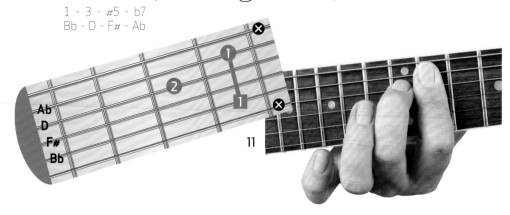

1   Bb7sus (Bb7sus4)

1 - 4 - 5 - b7
Bb - Eb - F - Ab

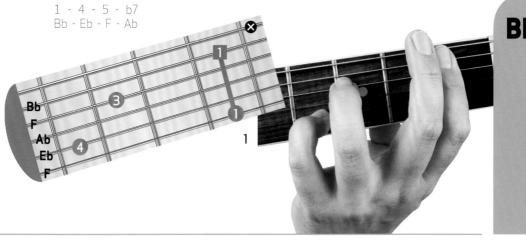

2   Bb7sus (Bb7sus4)

1 - 4 - 5 - b7
Bb - Eb - F - Ab

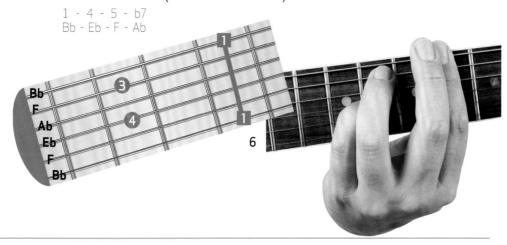

3   Bb7sus (Bb7sus4)

1 - 4 - 5 - b7
Bb - Eb - F - Ab

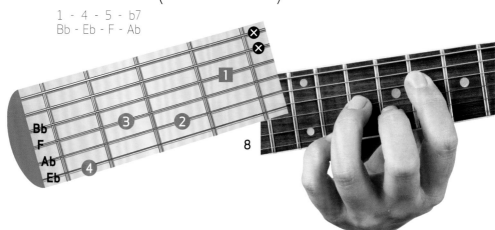

Bb7

Dominant seventh chords can be "extended" by stacking additional intervals such as ninths and thirteenths on top of the basic four-note chord. **Bb7#9** This voicing incorporates the open fourth string for extra resonance. **Bb13: 1** Sixth string "root" voicing with the fifth and ninth intervals omitted but still retaining a distinct "thirteenth" quality.

Bb9 (Bbdom9)

1 - 3 - 5 - b7 - 9
Bb - D - F - Ab - C

Bb7#9

1 - 3 - 5 - b7 - #9
Bb - D - F - Ab - C#

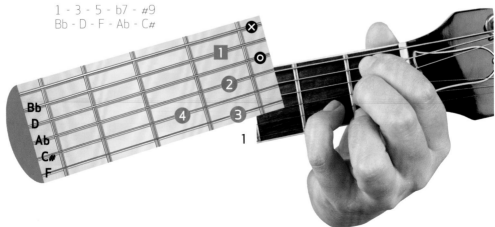

Bb7b9

1 - 3 - 5 - b7 - b9
Bb - D - F - Ab - Cb

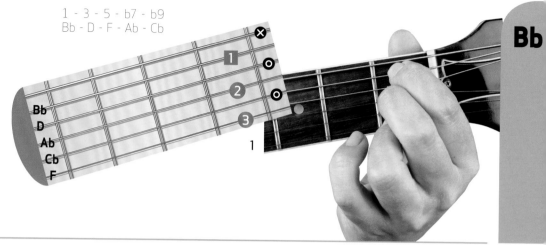

1

Bb13

1 - 3 - 5 - b7 - 9 - 13
Bb - D - F - Ab - C - G

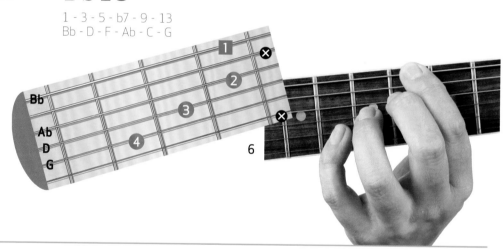

2

Bb13

1 - 3 - 5 - b7 - 9 - 13
Bb - D - F - Ab - C - G

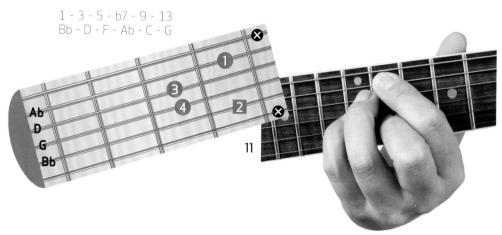

B MAJOR

Although only chord IV (E) is available as an open chord, and the key signature contains five sharps, B major is nonetheless a popular key. The lack of an open B chord does not stop the fretted versions sounding full and resonant. **3** The big six-string, full barre voicing that's great for a full strummed rhythm sound.

1   B (Bmaj, Bmajor, BM)

1 - 3 - 5
B - D# - F#

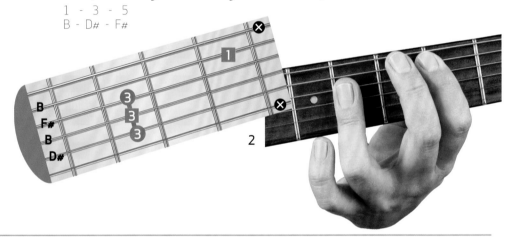

2   B (Bmaj, Bmajor, BM)

1 - 3 - 5
B - D# - F#

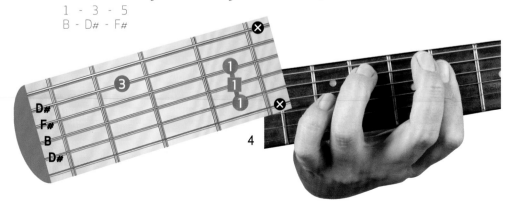

3 B (Bmaj, Bmajor, BM)

1 - 3 - 5
B - D# - F#

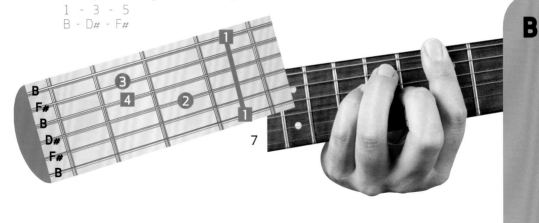

4 B (Bmaj, Bmajor, BM)

1 - 3 - 5
B - D# - F#

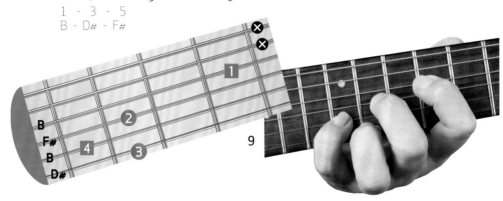

5 B (Bmaj, Bmajor, BM)

1 - 3 - 5
B - D# - F#

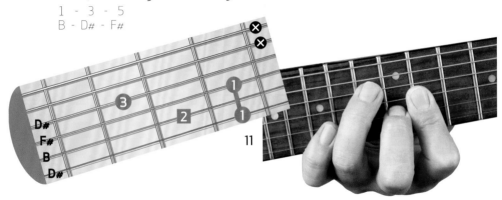

B

B MAJOR

Sixth chords add a major sixth to the basic major chord, hence their four-note (1 - 3 - 5 - 6) harmonic spelling. The five shapes below can be used as a substitute for any of the basic B major chords shown on pages 212–213.
1 First position voicing with open B-string included and doubled root for extra resonance. **3** A "closed" simple four-string voicing with no doubled notes.

1
B6 (Bmaj6, Bmajor6, BM6)
1 - 3 - 5 - 6
B - D# - F# - G#

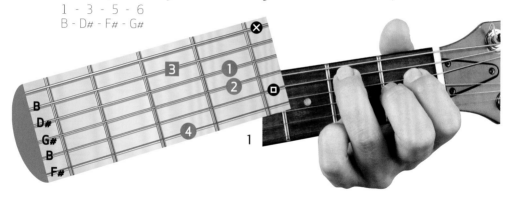

2
B6 (Bmaj6, Bmajor6, BM6)
1 - 3 - 5 - 6
B - D# - F# - G#

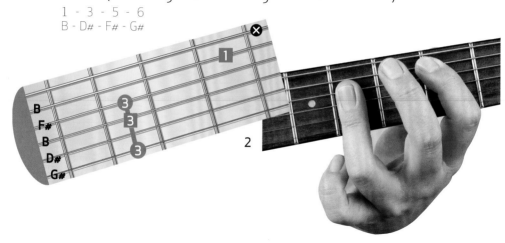

3 B6 (Bmaj6, Bmajor6, BM6)

1 - 3 - 5 - 6
B - D# - F# - G#

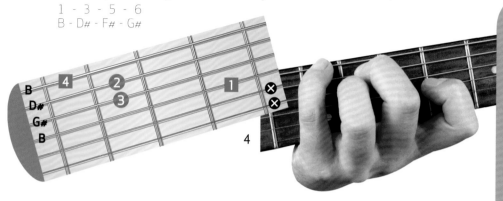

4 B6 (Bmaj6, Bmajor6, BM6)

1 - 3 - 5 - 6
B - D# - F# - G#

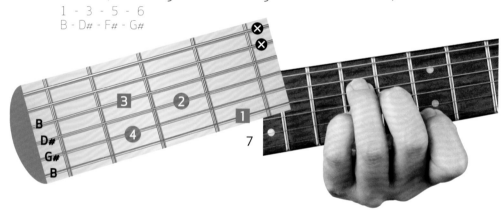

5 B6 (Bmaj6, Bmajor6, BM6)

1 - 3 - 5 - 6
B - D# - F# - G#

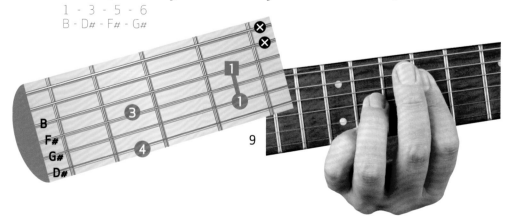

B

B MAJOR

The major seventh chord has a smooth and sophisticated sound that is often associated with jazz but can also be used in many other genres.
1 An unusual voicing that uses the open B-string to add a dash of chromatic dissonance—try this chord with a lush chorus effect.
4 Four-note "closed" voicing for a pure and simple major seventh sound.

1 ## Bmaj7 (B△, Bmajor7, BM7)
1 - 3 - 5 - 7
B - D# - F# - A#

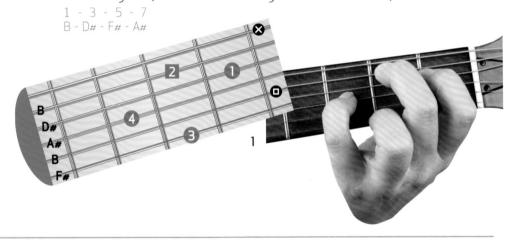

2 ## Bmaj7 (B△, Bmajor7, BM7)
1 - 3 - 5 - 7
B - D# - F# - A#

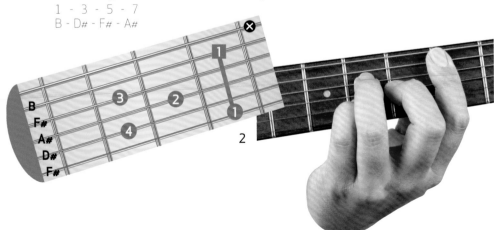

3   Bmaj7 (B△, Bmajor7, BM7)

1 - 3 - 5 - 7
B - D# - F# - A#

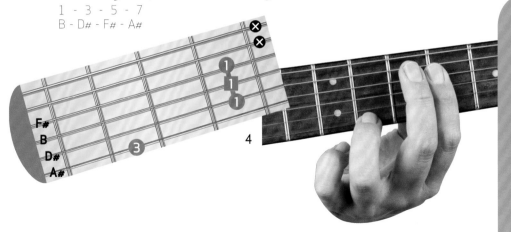

4   Bmaj7 (B△, Bmajor7, BM7)

1 - 3 - 5 - 7
B - D# - F# - A#

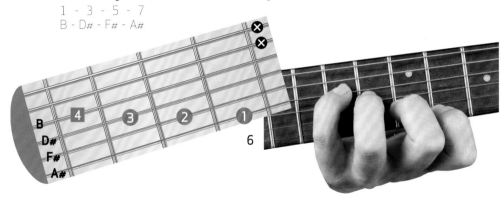

5   Bmaj7 (B△, Bmajor7, BM7)

1 - 3 - 5 - 7
B - D# - F# - A#

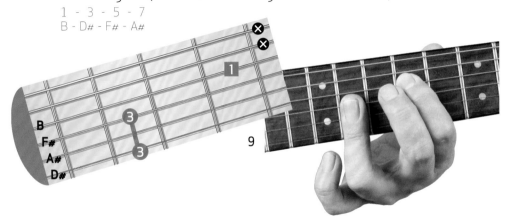

B

B MAJOR
Bsus (B suspended)

Because they contain no third, suspended chords are frequently used to create harmonic ambiguity, since they are technically neither major nor minor.
Bsus2: 2 High-register, four-note chord with doubled root—ideal for creating a big sound in a twin guitar rhythm section.
Bsus4: 2 Full six-string barre that can be used with B major, shape 1 on page 213 to create exciting rhythm parts.

1 Bsus2

1 - 2 - 5
B - C# - F#

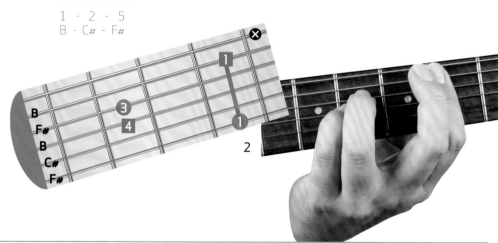

2 Bsus2

1 - 2 - 5
B - C# - F#

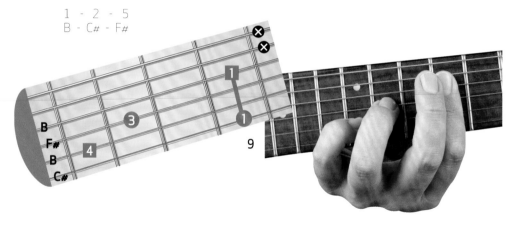

1 # Bsus4
1 - 4 - 5
B - E - F#

2 # Bsus4
1 - 4 - 5
B - E - F#

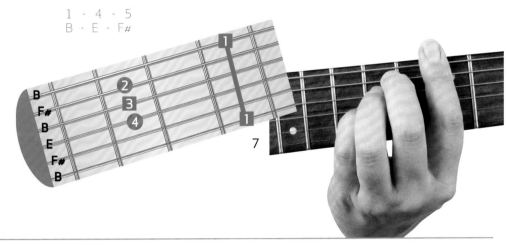

3 # Bsus4
1 - 4 - 5
B - E - F#

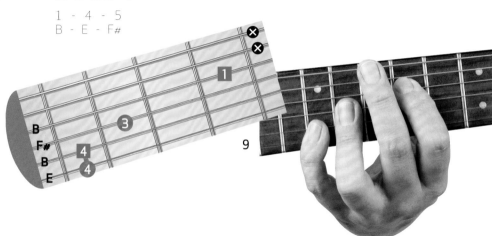

B MINOR

The key of B minor is the relative minor key of D major (key signature: two sharps) and is a popular guitar key. Descending bass lines with arpeggiated chords are easy to create utilizing the open fifth string (this works best when using shape 1 below)—consequently many rock ballads and slower tempo songs have been written in this key.

1

Bm (Bmin, Bminor, B–)

1 - b3 - 5
B - D - F#

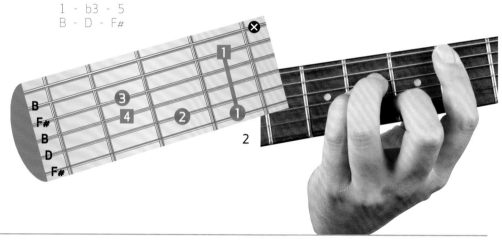

2

Bm (Bmin, Bminor, B–)

1 - b3 - 5
B - D - F#

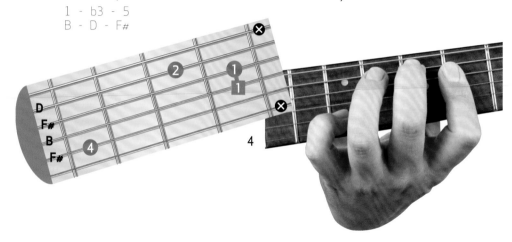

3 ## Bm (Bmin, Bminor, B–)

1 - b3 - 5
B - D - F#

4 ## Bm (Bmin, Bminor, B–)

1 - b3 - 5
B - D - F#

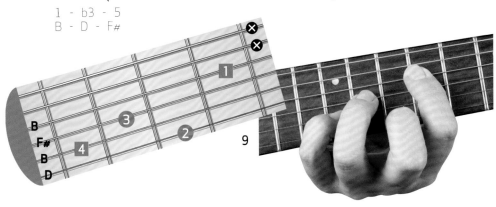

5 ## Bm (Bmin, Bminor, B–)

1 - b3 - 5
B - D - F#

B MINOR

Minor sixth chords can be used as a substitute for a simple minor chord when extra harmonic "color" is required (especially in static chords). Minor seventh chords can also be used to substitute a basic minor chord but are more frequently used as the first chord of a II - V - I progression.

1 ## Bmin6 (Bminor6, Bm6, B−6)

1 - b3 - 5 - 6
B - D - F# - G#

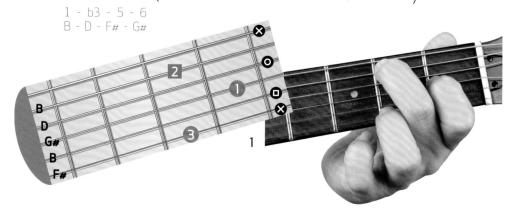

2 ## Bmin6 (Bminor6, Bm6, B−6)

1 - b3 - 5 - 6
B - D - F# - G#

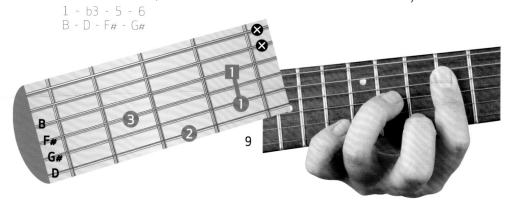

1   # Bmin7 (Bminor7, Bm7, B–7)

1 - b3 - 5 - b7
B - D - F# - A

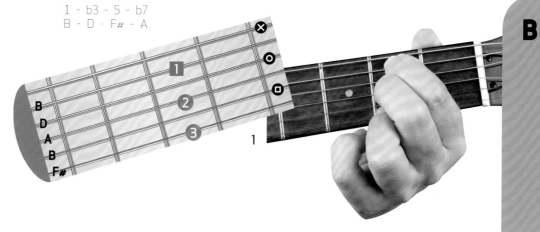

2   # Bmin7 (Bminor7, Bm7, B–7)

1 - b3 - 5 - b7
B - D - F# - A

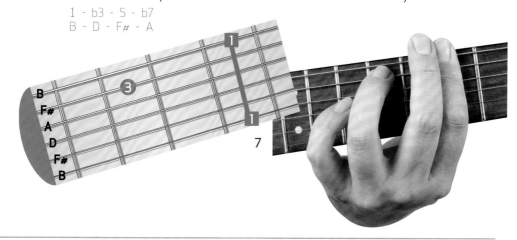

3   # Bmin7 (Bminor7, Bm7, B–7)

1 - b3 - 5 - b7
B - D - F# - A

B7

Since B major has such a resonant sound it is hardly surprising that many great blues have been written and played in this key. For a perfect example of just how good a blues in B major can sound, listen to Jimi Hendrix's virtuoso playing on "Red House" (from his seminal 1967 album *Are You Experienced*).

1

B7 (Bdom7)

1 - 3 - 5 - b7
B - D# - F# - A

2

B7 (Bdom7)

1 - 3 - 5 - b7
B - D# - F# - A

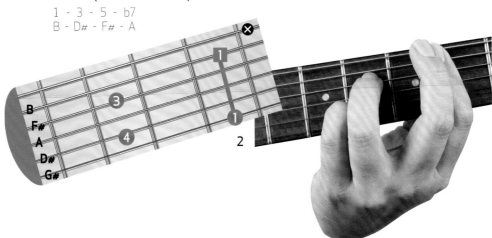

3   B7 (Bdom7)

1 - 3 - 5 - b7
B - D# - F# - A

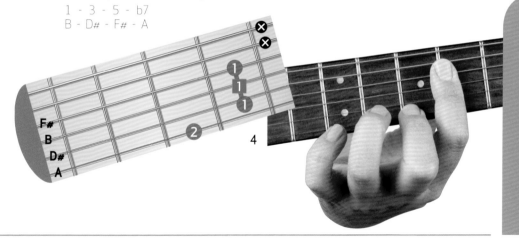

B

4   B7 (Bdom7)

1 - 3 - 5 - b7
B - D# - F# - A

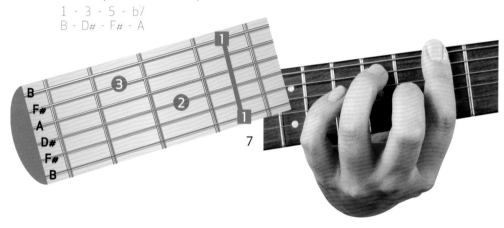

5   B7 (Bdom7)

1 - 3 - 5 - b7
B - D# - F# - A

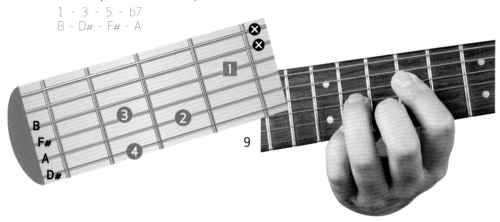

B7

To create extra tension within a perfect cadence (V–I) a sharpened fifth is often added to the dominant seventh chord. Suspended dominant chords suggest less harmonic movement and so can be used to add extra interest to static chords or vamps.

B7#5: 1 Basic open B7 chord with top voice raised a half-step to create the "sharp five" sound.

B7sus: 2 The full six-string barre variant for when a big-sounding chord is required.

1 B7#5 (B7aug, B7+)

1 - 3 - #5 - b7
B - D# - F## - A

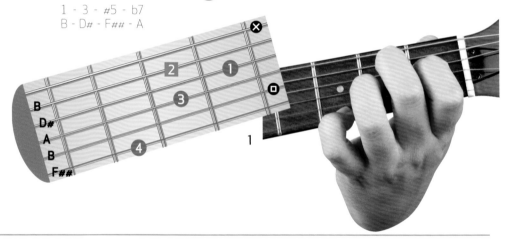

2 B7#5 (B7aug, B7+)

1 - 3 - #5 - b7
B - D# - F## - A

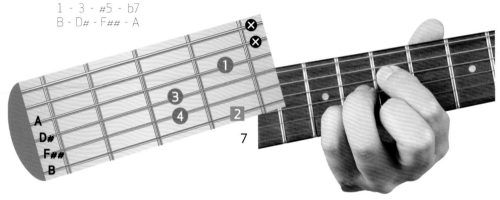

1   B7sus (B7sus4)

1 - 4 - 5 - b7
B - E - F# - A

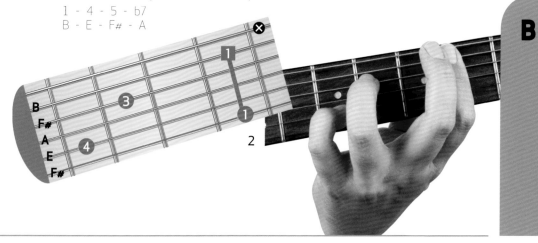

2   B7sus (B7sus4)

1 - 4 - 5 - b7
B - E - F# - A

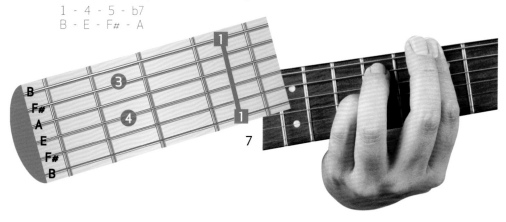

3   B7sus (B7sus4)

1 - 4 - 5 - b7
B - E - F# - A

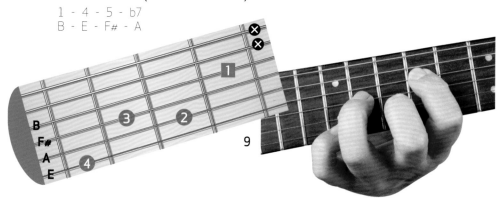

B

B7

These five shapes are all either "ninth" or "thirteen" variations of the dominant seventh chord and have a more sophisticated sound than the basic four-note chord.

B7#9 Situated low on the neck in first position, this four-note chord (with fifth omitted) has a big, bluesy sound.

B13: 1 Another voicing with no fifth, this time a five-note, resonant thirteenth chord.

● ## B9 (Bdom9)
1 - 3 - 5 - b7 - 9
B - D# - F# - A - C#

● ## B7#9
1 - 3 - 5 - b7 - #9
B - D# - F# - A - C##

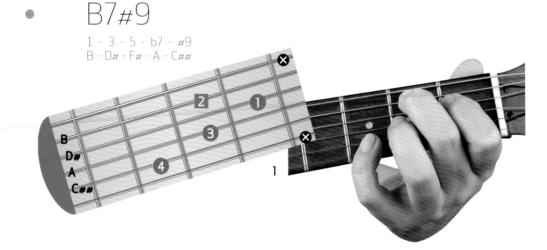

● ## B7b9
1 - 3 - 5 - b7 - b9
B - D# - F# - A - C

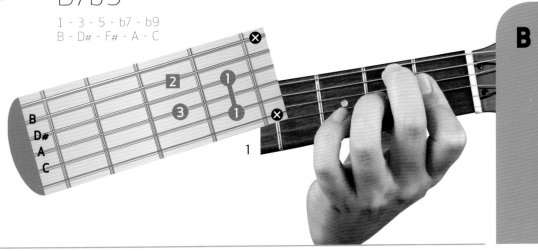

B

1 ## B13
1 - 3 - 5 - b7 - 9 - 13
B - D# - F# - A - C# - G#

2 ## B13
1 - 3 - 5 - b7 - 9 - 13
B - D# - F# - A - C# - G#

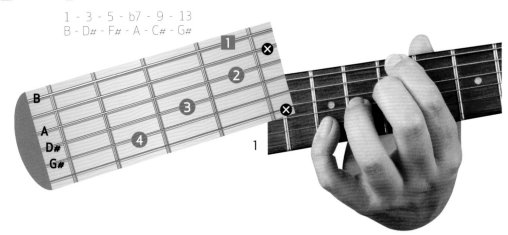

CHORD SUPPLEMENTS

Section 2

ROCK
Open Power Chords

Power chords are basically chords that sound great when played loud through a cranked-up valve amp. No other instrument can replicate that sound—it is truly the exclusive domain of the electric guitar. These chords are called "five" chords because they contain no third, just a root and a fifth. The bracketed notes in the following examples are the root notes doubled an octave higher and can be added for an even bigger sound if desired.

1   E5

1 - 5
E - B

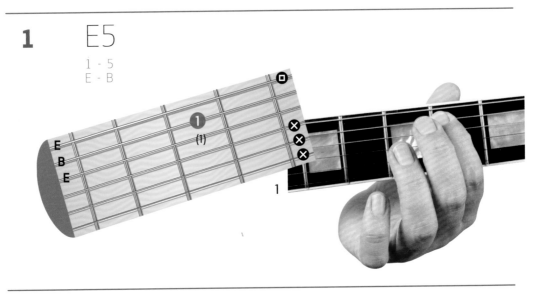

2   E5

1 - 5
E - B

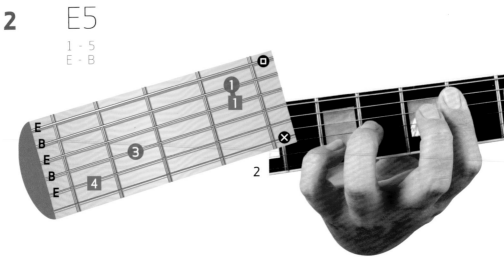

A5

1 - 5
A - E

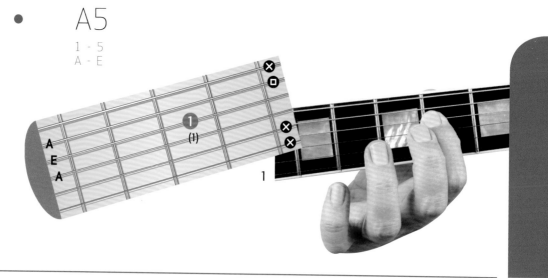

D5

1 - 5
D - A

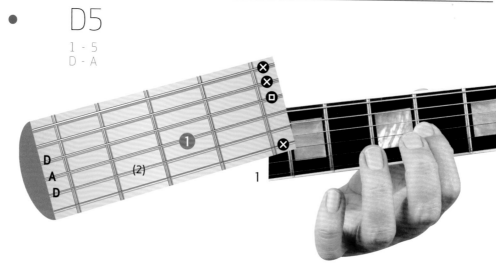

G5

1 - 5
G - D

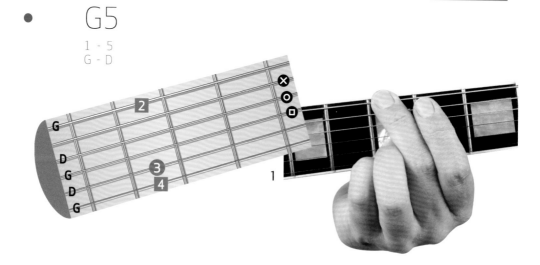

ROCK
Moveable Power Chords

These moveable power chord shapes can be played anywhere on the neck; the higher register voicings (shapes 1 and 2) are less resonant and often used in second guitar parts. Notice that shape 1 has the root note "on top" —this is the note that determines the root name of the chord (e.g. for B5 simply shift the shape down a half-step).

1   C5

1 - 5
C - G

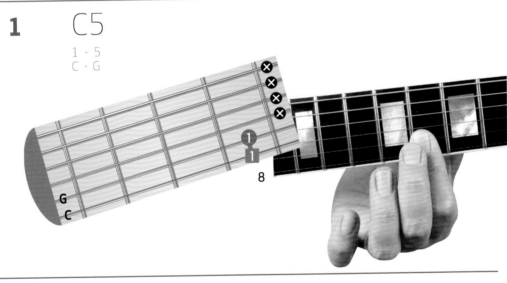

2   C5

1 - 5
C - G

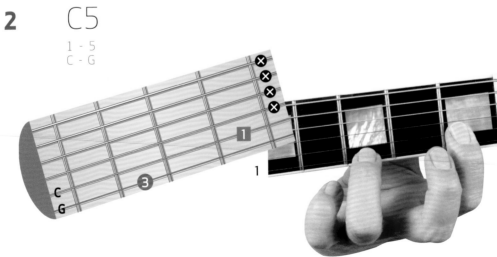

3   C5

1 - 5
C - G

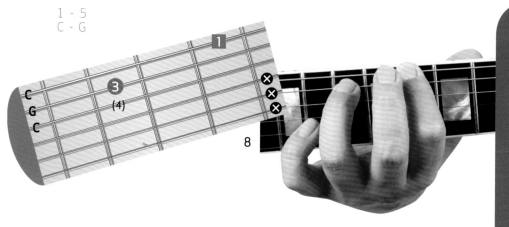

4   C5

1 - 5
C - G

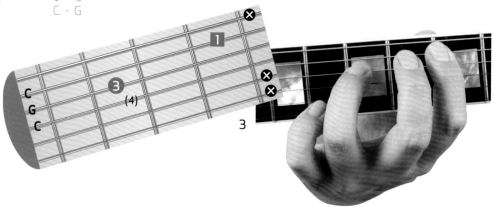

5   C5

1 - 5
C - G

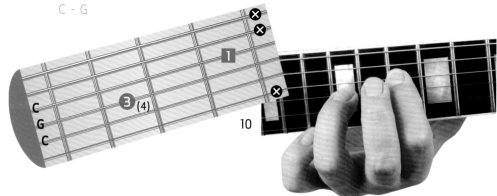

BLUES TO JAZZ
Three-Note Chords

The following selection of chords is comprised of only three notes—this makes the shapes easy to fret, so they are very useful when quick chord changes are required. You can also use these voicings when a less "dense" sound is required (for example, when playing with a keyboard player). Some of the voicings contain no root note: this is often omitted when playing in a rhythm section—it's the bass player's job to play the root!

1 C9

1 - 3 - 5 - b7 - 9
C - E - G - Bb - D

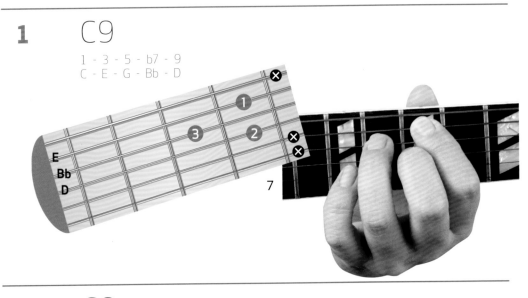

2 C9

1 - 3 - 5 - b7 - 9
C - E - G - Bb - D

1 C7

1 - 3 - 5 - b7
C - E - G - Bb

2 C7

1 - 3 - 5 - b7
C - E - G - Bb

3 C7

1 - 3 - 5 - b7
C - E - G - Bb

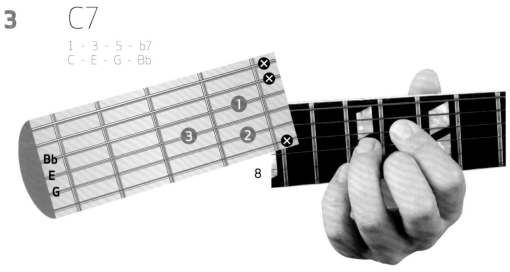

1 # Cmaj7
1 - 3 - 5 - 7
C - E - G - B

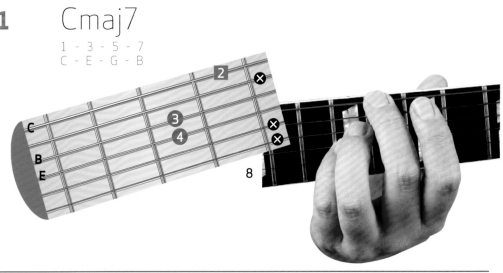

2 # Cmaj7
1 - 3 - 5 - 7
C - E - G - B

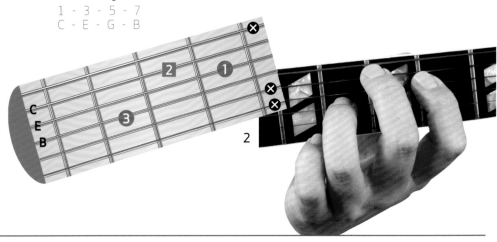

3 # Cmaj7
1 - 3 - 5 - 7
C - E - G - B

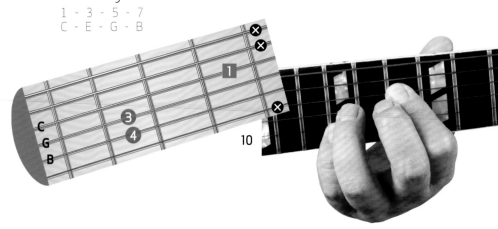

1 Cmin7

1 - b3 - 5 - b7
C - Eb - G - Bb

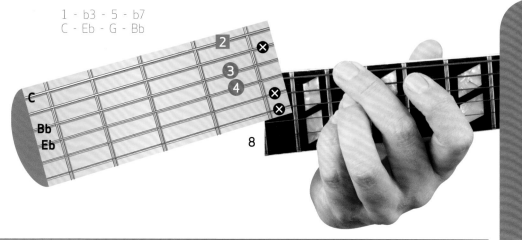

2 Cmin7

1 - b3 - 5 - b7
C - Eb - G - Bb

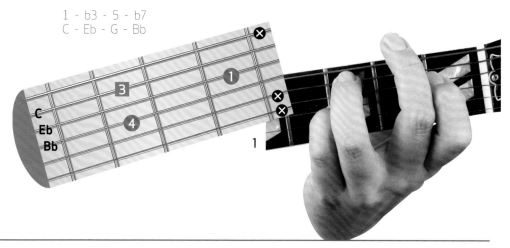

3 Cmin7

1 - b3 - 5 - b7
C - Eb - G - Bb

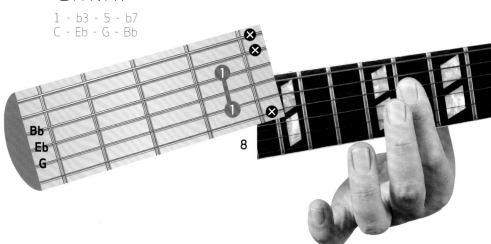

BLUES TO JAZZ
Multifunction Chords

These "multifunction" chords illustrate how one shape can be used for more than one chord type. This works best with three- or four-note chords; notice also that the root note is often omitted so these chords are really for rhythm section playing only—where you can rely on a bass player to add the root and complete the voicing.

1   ## Cm9

1 - b3 - 5 - b7 - 9
C - Eb - G - Bb - D

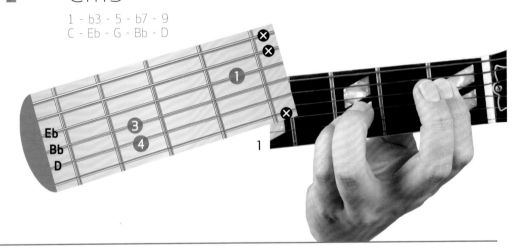

2   ## F13sus

1 - 4 - 5 - b7 - 9 - 13
F - Bb - C - Eb - G - D

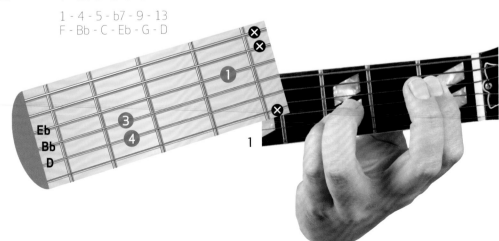

1 ## Cm6/9
1 - b3 - 5 - 6 - 9
C - Eb - G - A - D

2 ## F13
1 - 3 - 5 - b7 - 9 - 13
F - A - C - Eb - G - D

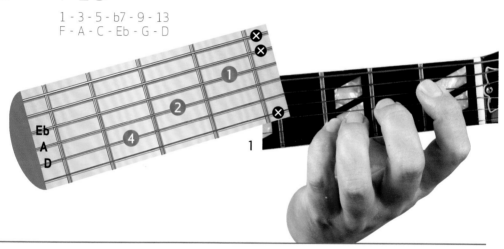

3 ## B7#9
1 - b3 - 5 - b7 - #9
B - D# - F# - A - C##

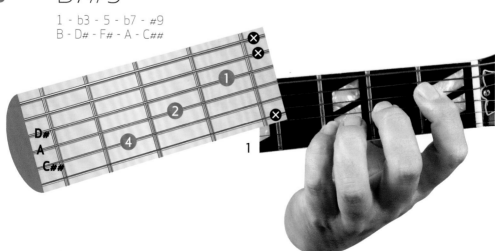

1   Cm7b5 (CØ)

1 - b3 - b5 - b7
C - Eb - Gb - Bb

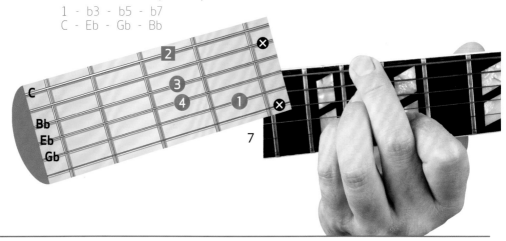

2   Ab9

1 - 3 - 5 - b7 - 9
Ab - C - Eb - Gb - Bb

3   D7#5b9

1 - 3 - #5 - b7 - b9
D - F# - A# - C - Eb

1 Cm7b5 (CØ)

1 - b3 - b5 - b7
C - Eb - Gb - Bb

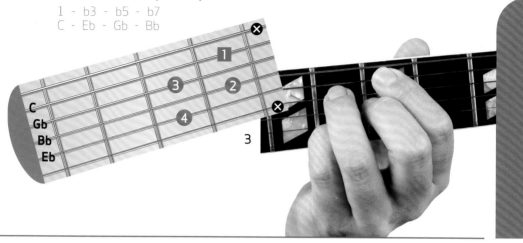

2 Ab9

1 - 3 - 5 - b7 - 9
Ab - C - Eb - Gb - Bb

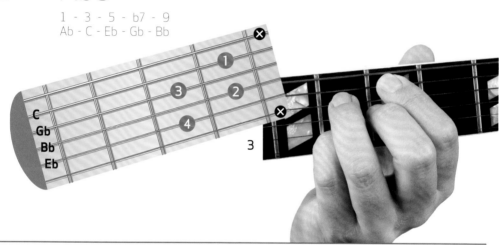

3 D7#5b9

1 - 3 - #5 - b7 - b9
D - F# - A# - C - Eb

1   Cm7b5 (CØ)

1 - b3 - b5 - b7
C - Eb - Gb - Bb

2   Ab9

1 - 3 - 5 - b7 - 9
Ab - C - Eb - Gb - Bb

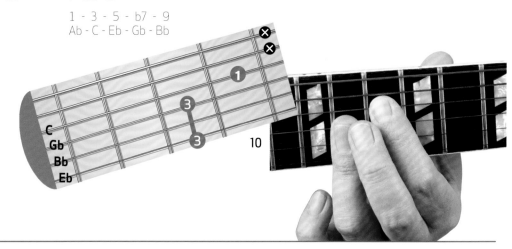

3   D7#5b9

1 - 3 - #5 - b7 - b9
D - F# - A# - C - Eb

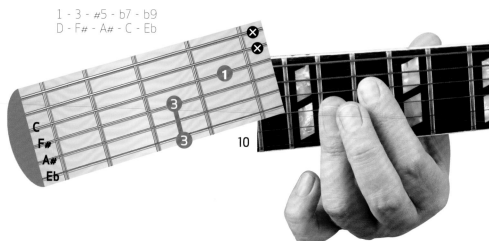

1 Cm11b5 (CØ)

1 - b3 - b5 - b7 - 9 - 11
C - Eb - Gb - Bb - D - F

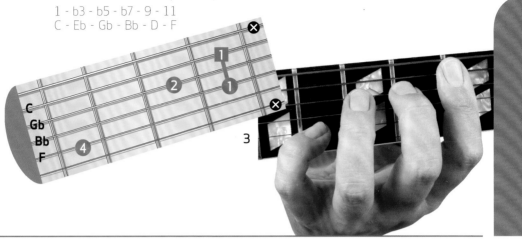

2 Ab13

1 - 3 - 5 - b7 - 9 - 11
Ab - C - Eb - Gb - Bb - F

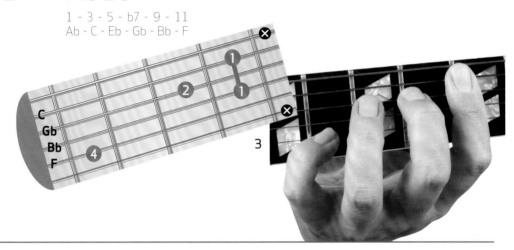

3 D7#5#9

1 - 3 - #5 - b7 - #9
D - F# - A# - C - E#

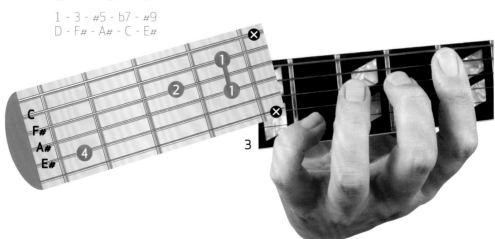

BLUES TO JAZZ
Diminished Chords

Diminished chords frequently occur as "chromatic passing chords" primarily in blues and jazz. However, they can also be used as a substitute for a dominant seventh "flat nine" chord (especially the four-note shapes opposite)—just play the lowest note a half-step above the seventh chord's root (e.g. shape 2 on page 247 could be used as a B7b9 chord).

1 ## C° (C°7, Cdim, C diminished)

1 - b3 - b5
C - Eb - Gb

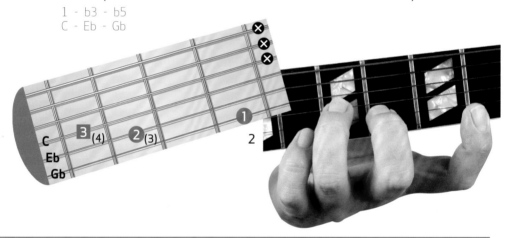

2 ## C° (C°7, Cdim, C diminished)

1 - b3 - b5
C - Eb - Gb

3 C° (C°7, Cdim, C diminished)

1 - b3 - b5 - b7
C - Eb - Gb - Bbb

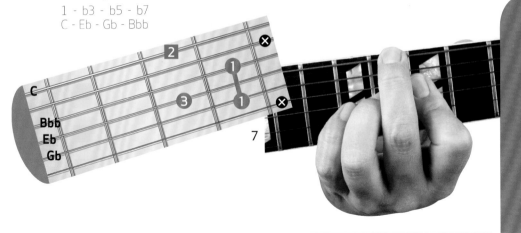

4 C° (C°7, Cdim, C diminished)

1 - b3 - b5 - b7
C - Eb - Gb - Bbb

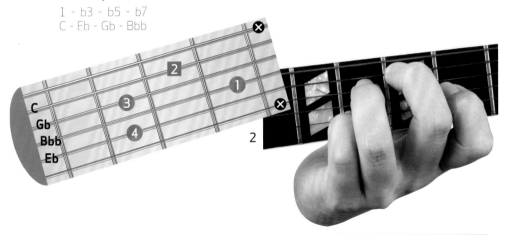

5 C° (C°7, Cdim, C diminished)

1 - b3 - b5 - b7
C - Eb - Gb - Bbb

SOUL, FUNK, AND REGGAE

All of the chords in this section are three-note voicings, and all are played on the top three strings of the guitar. This makes them ideal for the "chips" style of rhythm playing (short, staccato chord stabs) made famous by the great Stax guitarist and songwriter Steve Cropper. Many of these chords contain no root note—they will not describe the chord correctly without a bass player playing the low root.

1   C7 (Cdom9)

1 - 3 - 5 - b7
C - E - G - Bb

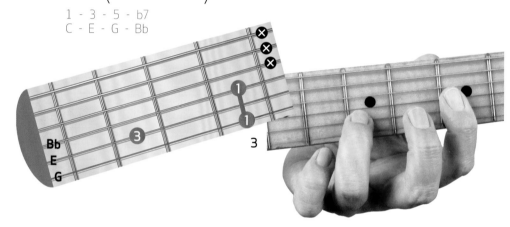

2   C7 (Cdom9)

1 - 3 - 5 - b7
C - E - G - Bb

C9

1 - 3 - 5 - b7 - 9
C - E - G - Bb - D

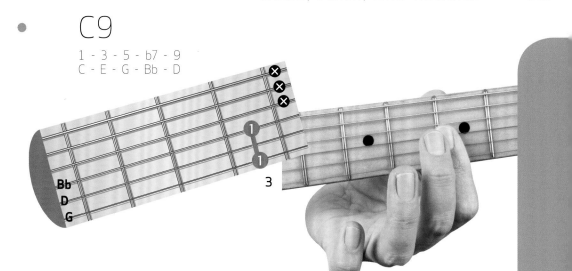

Bb
D
G

C13

1 - 3 - 5 - b7 - 9 - 13
C - E - G - Bb - D - A

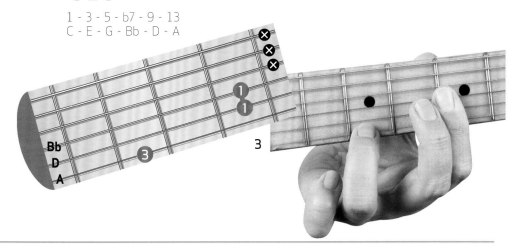

Bb
D
A

C7#9

1 - 3 - 5 - b7 - #9
C - E - G - Bb - D#

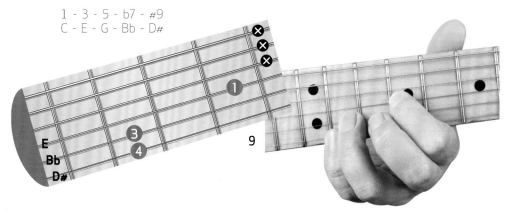

E
Bb
D#

1   C (Cmaj, C major, CM)

1 - 3 - 5
C - E - G

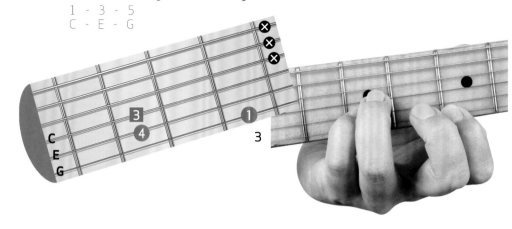

2   C (Cmaj, C major, CM)

1 - 3 - 5
C - E - G

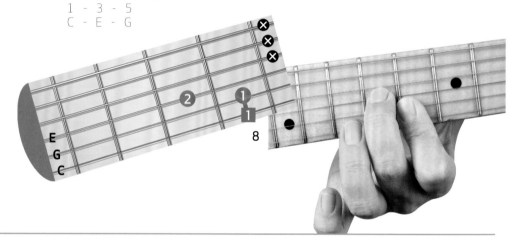

3   C (Cmaj, C major, CM)

1 - 3 - 5
C - E - G

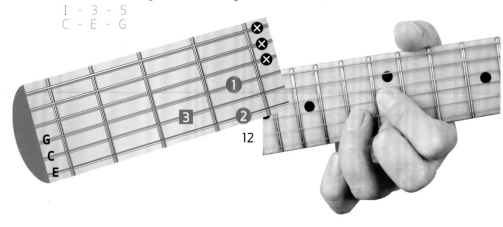

1 Cmaj7 (C△, C major7, CM7)

1 - 3 - 5 - 7
C - E - G - B

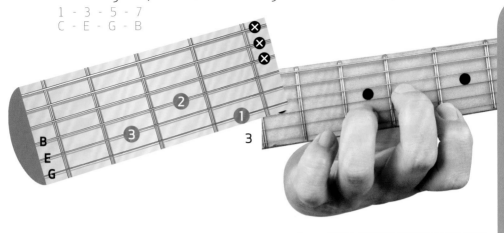

2 Cmaj7 (C△, C major7, CM7)

1 - 3 - 5 - 7
C - E - G - B

3 Cmaj7 (C△, C major7, CM7)

1 - 3 - 5 - 7
C - E - G - B

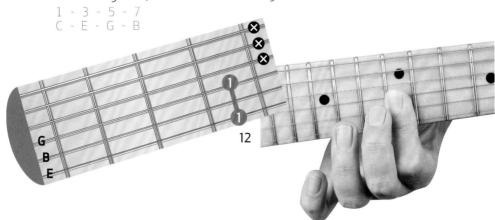

1   ## Cm (Cmin, C minor, C–)

1 - b3 - 5
C - Eb - G

2   ## Cm (Cmin, C minor, C–)

1 - b3 - 5
C - Eb - G

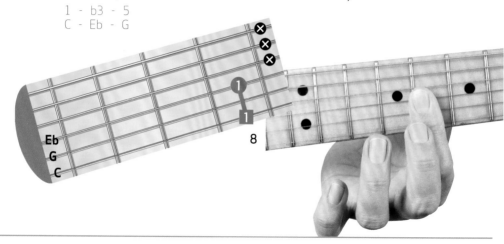

3   ## Cm (Cmin, C minor, C–)

1 - b3 - 5
C - Eb - G

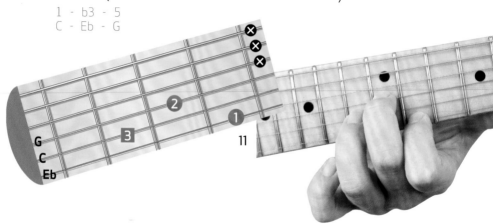

1   ## Cm7 (Cmin7, C minor7, C–7)

1 - b3 - 5 - b7
C - Eb - G - Bb

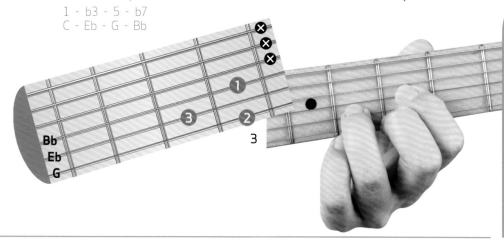

2   ## Cm7 (Cmin7, C minor7, C–7)

1 - b3 - 5 - b7
C - Eb - G - Bb

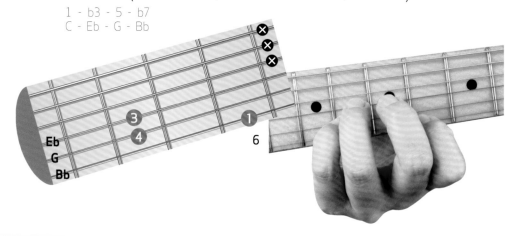

3   ## Cm7 (Cmin7, C minor7, C–7)

1 - b3 - 5 - b7
C - Eb - G - Bb

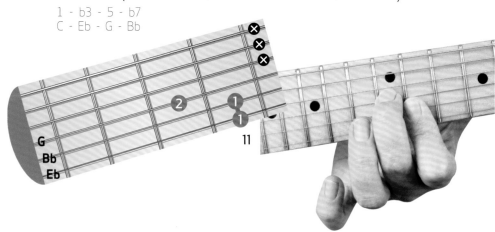

INDEX

CREDITS

Quarto would like to thank and acknowledge the following for supplying illustrations and photographs reproduced in this book: